You Can Be a Great Boss!

Everyone Deserves a Great Boss – Here's How to Become One

By
Jim D. Wilhelm, Ed.D.

"Don't pick a job. Pick a Boss. Your first boss is the biggest factor in your career success. A boss who doesn't trust you won't give you opportunities to grow."
--William Raduchel

Table of Contents

1. You Got the Promotion! What Now?   6
   The Importance of Training
   No Tunnel Vision Allowed
   Things To Do After Your First Promotion
2. Time for a New Skill Set   20
   Types of Skill Sets
   Learn New Approaches
   Balance is Key
   A Closer Look at Maslow's Hierarchy of Needs
   Equity Theory Defined
   Can You Truly Motivate Others?
   McClelland's Human Motivation Theory

3. Where Does Your Power Come From?   48
   Sources of Power
   Management vs Leadership
4. Poor Bosses: We've All Had Them   53
   Human Relations is at the Heart of Everything
   Signs You Have a Terrible Boss
   Bad Bosses Infect the Workplace
   An American Tragedy
   What To Do When You Have a Bad Boss
5. The Peter Principle is Valid   82
   How the Peter Principle Works
   The Peter Principle in Action
   Overcoming the Peter Principle
   Applying the Peter Principle Test
   Tips for First-Time Managers
   Why the Peter Principle Works
6. What's Your Leadership Style?   99
   The Leadership Grid
   Situational Leadership
   Theory X and Theory Y
   Theory Z
   What about Theory W?
7. The Evidence Is In! Great Companies Have Great Bosses!   112
   What Makes a Company a Great Place to Work?
   Traits of Great Bosses
   If You Want to be a Good Boss, Be a Good Leader
   Great Companies Lead the Way
8. I Can't Function This Way!   126
   Top 10 Reasons to Quit Your Job
   Other Signs It's Time to Leave
   You've Decided to Leave, Now Comes the Exit Interview
9. Final Summary   145

Introduction

I wrote this book because of all of the poor bosses I've had who were not qualified for their position or who seemed to never learn people skills. Maybe they were promoted because they were related to someone in the company or they played office politics well. Who knows? However, the problem is not necessarily how they got there, but that they are now in a position of authority, which can spell disaster for their employees and the company. It's obvious that a bad boss can do much more damage than a bad employee. It is my hope that this book will help aspiring bosses learn to be great bosses and that employees will benefit by being motivated to grow in and out of their organizations.

Why don't organizations invest in management training programs? It would seem to be a no-brainer to want to perpetuate excellence by employing and maintaining good employees. Many companies do just that, but the concern lies in the companies that don't train their employees thoroughly to allow them to grow and succeed. Many times we've been told that we will be trained for a certain period of time and then management throws us into the job in half that time. They usually cite an unforeseen circumstance such as someone quit suddenly or retired or was terminated. This is a disservice to the employee who then must "self-train," picking up bad habits along the way that will later have to be corrected. As we'll discuss, poorly trained bosses hurt the company and the employees in all sorts of ways: lower productivity, lower morale, higher turnover, and stress-related health problems, to name a few.

This book emphasizes the "training" aspect to develop good employees, thus resulting in good bosses. We will discuss the newly promoted manager needing a new skill set and where his or her power comes from. This will lead us to examples of poor bosses, explanation of the Peter Principle, and reviewing leadership styles. We will emphasize motivation theories because great bosses know how to motivate employees. We'll make the case for great companies having great bosses, (and they do exist). Finally, there will be suggestions as to what to do if you've tried and tried, but decide it's best to leave the company.

This book will assist you in first becoming a great employee, and then help you work your way up to becoming a great boss!

About the Author

Jim Wilhelm has a B.B.A., M.S., and an Ed.D from Texas Tech University. He's worked for General Motors, Farmers Insurance, been self-employed, and has taught Business, Speech, and Math courses at South Plains College, Lubbock, TX. Wilhelm has been teaching for over 30 years. He worked as a trainer for AT&T, traveled the West Coast training GM dealers, and taught for Southwestern Public Service Company. Wilhelm has authored the following books: *Human Relations IS Your Business, So You Want to be a Community College Teacher,* and *In-Your-Face Human Relations.*

1. You Got the Promotion! What Now?

Congratulations! The company has finally recognized your talent and potential and rewarded you with a promotion to management! This is what you've been working towards for years, ever since you started with the company. Now, the day has finally come when all of your hard work has paid off. But what happens now? Will you go to a management training seminar? Will you be working with a mentor, or will you have to fend for yourself? How will you be trained, or will you be? What's the next step?

Many surveys reveal that over 50% of Americans have quit a job to get away from their manager. A lot of workers quit the *boss*, not the *company*. Further research shows that anywhere from 50-70% of us are disengaged from work. This is due, mostly, from poor supervisors. Workers who are disengaged at work create such problems as: higher turnover, higher accident rates, lower productivity, lower morale, and increased absenteeism. A disengaged employee spreads negativity throughout the organization.

The Importance of Training
Despite it being a significant career change from their individual work, most companies provide little to no training for their managers. What training they do get is often packed into a single day long training seminar. These are often inspiring and motivating, but often retention is poor as they're overwhelmed with ideas, and sometimes distracted by work demands. Knowing this, is it any surprise many struggle with their management responsibilities? Many bad bosses become that way, because no one taught them what they should do. (http://fractio.nl/2014/09/19/not-a-promotion-a-career-change/)

A lot of companies do have some sort of management training program whether it's sending you to a training seminar or simply having you shadow another manager to learn the ropes. Unfortunately, not all companies take the time to train new managers properly and when they don't; the organization is setting itself up for employee turnover, complaints, morale problems, and managers who have no propensity to lead. This manifests itself through power plays, building empires, and playing politics, the result being a poor manager, who is sometimes even hated. It's tragic, but it happens all too often. One axiom for organizations to remember is that a technical superstar may not make for a good manager. Examples include an NBA superstar who retires and is hired as a coach. Or, an excellent, caring teacher may get promoted into administration. Of course, it should increase the likelihood of them being effective managers (or coaches), but it doesn't always play out that way. When I started teaching Math I was forced into taking a new perspective. I always enjoyed working math problems and I would take short-cuts to solve problems. However, knowing a subject and teaching that subject to others is totally different. If you're very good at what you do, it often doesn't translate into helping others achieve that same level of productivity and efficiency. A different perspective is required and this emphasizes the importance of training. It prevents the new manager from developing bad habits that will be harder to overcome later on. If the company had taken the time to train them initially, it would save a lot of heartache and frustration on down the line for everyone.

One reason management training is so vital is because the employee has, heretofore, had a *worms eye* perspective at work (doing day-to-day job assignments) and then when they are elevated to a management position they must shift to more of a *birds eye* perspective. What they say and decisions they make are of more importance now because more people are listening. A management position is more conceptual in nature than technical and the overall view of the company must now be considered. The gripe sessions with coworkers and gossiping for enjoyment are over and you must now be more professional in your stance. You may have to explain policies or procedures to subordinates and justify them from the company perspective. No more second-guessing, especially in front of the people you supervise. In a nutshell, you're no longer responsible for just yourself. There are other people involved, so a bad decision on your part can have far-reaching implications. It's a transition. It's a huge transition!

I once had a manager who would meet with us and say something like, "I don't agree with the decision, but upper management says we have to..." In my opinion, this was a terrible technique because while you're trying to paint the picture that you know better than upper management, you're actually discounting the decision and causing doubt and dissension in your employees. As a new boss, it has now become your responsibility to convey management decisions to your subordinates in a unified manner and you need to put your personal opinions in your pocket. You must get onboard to help others accept the change or decision that was made from higher up. Second-guessing a superior should be done only with that superior, not broadcast to everyone to show you would have made a better decision. It makes management look bad and it makes you look even worse.

You will also no longer be leaving at five o'clock. Work will follow you home because you're a manager 24 hours a day. As a regular employee, your only worries were doing your job well, and you left it at the office at 5 o'clock to go about your personal life. However, your promotion to management has changed all of that. You'll be thinking ahead to the next day and worrying about quotas and agendas. Will you be short-handed again tomorrow, or is Bill returning after his illness? Do you need to hire a new employee? Does someone need to be put on probation or terminated? When will you train the new hire? These sorts of concerns will be on your mind. (We will talk about work-life balance later). Being a good manager takes hard work, practice, and determination. The reward is that you are a leader! You now have the power to influence!

If you work for a larger company, your promotion will probably be accompanied by a move to another branch office because it gives you a fresh start and you will be viewed as a manager from day one. In smaller companies, it could be harder to move to being a manager because your coworkers suddenly become your subordinates. That's not saying you can't be a successful manager in a smaller company and it may be helpful that you know your subordinates. However, sometimes there is no choice and a smaller company may have no branch office, which is the nature of smaller organizations. That's fine and everyone understands that. The people you work with can be very supportive of you knowing that you deserved the promotion. On the other hand, those who weren't promoted may have some resentment. But, again, it is a transition and employees need to respect your authority. It changes perspectives and perceptions for both the manager and the employees.

When I finished my doctorate, it was frowned upon to turn around and be employed as a professor at that same university (I don't think they had a written policy). Why? Because you're still viewed as a doctoral student by your peers and it may be a struggle for a newly minted "doctor" to receive the respect and recognition deserved. However, when you move to another university you're viewed as an equal starting with the first day of the semester.

Relationships will change. They won't necessarily change for better or worse, they will just be different. You'll act more professional and you can continue attending happy hour on Friday's, but excuse yourself after one drink and give your employees room to breathe and vent. After all, happy hour is a time to de-stress and discuss the workweek without the boss being around. It's also a bonding time, because it is just as important as the company picnic or the bowling team. It helps validate employees' worth while giving them a feeling of belonging and being part of the team and company. If you stay past one drink you will inevitably inhibit employees from discussing their workweek and happy hour Friday's may fall apart (or be moved without your knowledge). The key is to let employees know you enjoy their company outside of work, but don't overstay your welcome. There's no law against being boss and continuing to maintain friendships.

We are all composites of people we've known. As a teacher, I've molded my teaching style from professors I've had before. I once had a professor for Business Law who actually read his entire dissertation to the class. (Even my mother never read my dissertation, but she kept it on the coffee table). It took the whole class period and no one understood how it related to our subject matter. The class was a "snoozer" and the whole semester we all fought boredom and tried to keep from falling asleep in class. We knew the exams were taken from the book, which he seldom covered, so we studied the book. No one listened to his droning in class and I vowed that when I began my teaching career that I would never be as boring as that B. Law professor.

Previously, and the reader can probably relate to this, high school history was usually taught by a coach who didn't seem to care much about the subject. He would read the book to us and I'm sure the class was a sidelight to his coaching because it was easy to observe that he didn't want to teach the course or even be in the classroom. By the same token, my college history professor was dynamic, animated, and enthusiastic (I hated history up to that point). He used voice inflection and re-enactments to keep students engaged and when class was over we couldn't wait to read the next chapter in the book to see what happened!

The point is, we've all had good and bad teachers and we know maximum learning requires students to be engaged. This is done through discussion, group work, relating a lesson to the real world, challenging students, and respecting and caring about them as people.

It is easy to draw the parallel between being a good teacher and being a good boss. Continuing in that vein, we've all had bad bosses. Bosses who are not qualified (it's who you know, not what you do), have no clue, or the power has gone to their head. If the boss isn't excited about work and task accomplishment, how can the employees be excited about their work? The boss sets the tone for a positive or negative work experience and it is imperative that they be motivated, positive role models for the people they supervise.

Throw yourself into your new position, but try to maintain work-life balance, too. Don't burnout. That's to say, you can't constantly work 12-hour days without getting out of balance. Everyone needs a break, everyone should take a vacation to refresh and regain perspective. It's so important to realize that there's more to life than work, work, work.

Certainly, there are times in your career when you may need to work longer hours initially to learn the job or to work on an important project, but it should be <u>short term</u>. When you focus too long on one thing, you lose yourself, and your work-life balance. There will come a point when the stress will break down your body and then what good are all of those extra hours you put in?

Another negative to working too much is if you continue to be a workaholic, then it's logical, after a period of time, when you don't get the recognition or big pay raise you feel you deserve, that you'll start thinking "all the nights and weekends I've spent here correcting others' mistakes, and this is the thanks I get!" That's usually when bitterness and resentment set in. Always try to maintain balance in your work and personal life and you'll not only be a better employee, but you'll also have a better life away from work.

<u>No Tunnel Vision Allowed</u>
Tunnel vision is where you, as manager, are so focused on following the rules and policies, for example, that you lose sight of the big picture. Remember, the total person approach is to look beyond one incident or event in an employee's life and realize that they are an excellent employee who is simply going through something short-term. A short-sighted approach may leave you short one employee.

Take, for example, my friend Julie, in Texas. She was an excellent employee with great performance evaluations, but she was battling breast cancer. She had been caring for her elderly parents when her father suddenly passed away, and, unfortunately, within two weeks her mother passed also. Julie was contending with her own serious illness and had used part of her vacation time on doctor and hospital visits. Without any warning, and with no compassion, her boss reprimanded her for taking too much time off work for personal and family issues.

Julie's story is a prime example of tunnel vision and lack of compassion, or empathy, by her boss. She was a hard worker who had been with the company for years, but rather than find ways to support her in challenging times, the boss chose a mindless adherence to company policy. The boss's lack of concern for Julie's situation spoke volumes to her and to other employees about company priorities.

A better approach would have focused on offering support to Julie and helping to find a solution. From that day forward she knew the boss was unfeeling and the level of trust between them began to deteriorate. The way the situation was handled reflected poorly on the company and employee morale was affected adversely. This is an example of how lack of support, or compassion, can be a factor in whether a boss is considered good or bad. In this case, the boss failed the test for being a good boss. However, it's also an example of the far-reaching consequences of managerial decisions and their impact on the whole organization.

Another example of tunnel vision comes to mind when my friend told me he almost got a traffic ticket because he didn't use his turn signal while driving one morning. He was approaching a one-way street in a residential neighborhood and could only turn right onto that one-way street (it was a t-intersection) so there was no need to use a turn signal. Immediately after he turned, a police officer pulled him over and said he hadn't used a turn signal. Bob isn't one to argue and wondered to himself why he would need to use a turn signal when there was only one way to proceed. Luckily, he received only a warning ticket. We both laughed about the incident later because this was an example of a cop with tunnel vision. He saw an intersection where a driver didn't use his turn signal, but if he had looked at the bigger picture, why would a turn signal be needed when there was only one direction to turn? While we guessed the officer was strictly enforcing traffic laws, we doubted it would have been upheld in court if my friend actually received a ticket. We figured it was either a rookie cop or an overzealous one.

Things To Do After Your First Promotion

- **No wholesale changes**. You're taking on new responsibilities and changing things around too fast may backfire on you. People will question what you're doing and your decision making will be second-guessed. Unless the company is in crisis mode where big changes must take place to avert disaster, take it slow and steady and get your feet on the ground first. There will be plenty of time to change things for the better. Incremental change is accepted more readily. This will also ease employees into trusting you instead of them gossiping the proverbial, "she doesn't know what she's doing and this change is silly." Try for small victories. If there's been an unnecessary policy or rule that everyone's been complaining about for a while then change it and you'll become a hero in their eyes.

- **What are your goals?** Taking time to write down your team or department goals will create a template for your planning. Also, writing down personal goals will be helpful. What do you want to accomplish with your team or department? Do you want to get rid of a lot of people who are nonperformers, or to train them better? Are you planning for a promotion within five years? How do the department goals support overall organizational goals?

- **Meet with everyone**. Meeting with employees individually sends the message that you care about them and begins to build rapport and trust. You'll want to establish a positive first impression and even though they know you, they don't know you as their boss. When you meet them, go to them; don't make them come to your office. This will set them at ease because you're on their turf and they will be more likely to open up to you. If, for some reason, you don't have time for individual consultations, then at least a group meeting would be helpful. The first meeting is about getting to know them and asking them their goals, save expectations or criticism for later. Try to pick the brains of other managers and learn from their experiences.

- **Use your human relations skills**. Respect them and they will do the same for you. If you go on a "power trip," and explain rules and regulations at your first meeting and that you're the boss now, it will start building walls between you and your subordinates. They'll come to dislike you and end up doing minimum work because you've ruined the work experience for them. The golden rule is a cliché but it's golden for a reason. If you were the subordinate, how would you like to be treated by a new boss?

- **Instill a team atmosphere**. Knowing you have the support of others can never be underestimated. Remain positive and help others realize they are part of a team and let them know that you care about them. Tell people you are human and that mistakes will be made, but those mistakes are learning tools to make the organization stronger. Emphasize that you will all grow together. Make a point of communicating with everyone frequently so they know what is going on in the organization. Timely communication is crucial.

Aretha Franklin said it best "R-E-S-P-E-C-T, find out what it means to me…" Everyone has something to teach you if you listen, so never speak down to anyone. Respecting other individuals will only enhance your position in the company.

Finally, even the bible supports being a good boss. "Nor yet as lording it over those allotted to your charge, but proving to be examples to the flock." (I Peter 5:3)

Summary

In summary, we've made the case that proper training is critical for employees, but even more so for successful managers. Training sets the tone for a person's career and instills in them confidence in the company that people care about them and want them to succeed. It also gives the employee the competence to do their job well.

Of course, no training, or poor training, lessens chances of success considerably. The employee flounders, develops bad habits, and generally takes a dim view of an organization that doesn't care to equip its people with the tools necessary to excel at their jobs. In turn, it negatively affects the organization in high turnover rates, inefficiency, poor communication, and ultimately, the bottom line. This is where you would think that companies would take immediate corrective action, but many don't.

As a new manager, you'll look at things differently because of more and varied responsibilities required of the position. Try to get your feet on the ground as soon as possible and learn the job duties before attempting big changes. Gaining the trust and confidence of your employees will lay the foundation for your future success as boss.

If for some reason the company didn't train you for your new position, and you want to stay with that company, then you'll essentially need to train yourself. Ask questions, find other bosses to assist you, and read management or leadership materials to develop your leadership style on your own. If you want to be a good boss, you will find a way to become one!

To be a great boss, try to model your behavior after the good bosses you've had. Many of us have had more bad bosses than good, which is okay. But learn from bad bosses as well and don't dwell on their bad behavior. Instead, use a positive perspective to move towards becoming a great boss, and not away from being a bad boss. Visualize yourself leading people to success and being well-liked and looked up to, and make that vision reality.

2. Time for a New Skill Set

A skill set is a particular category of knowledge, abilities, and experience necessary to perform a job. Specific skills set areas include human relations, research and planning, accounting, leadership, management, and computer skills. You can enhance your skill set to further your career progression.

Types of Skill Sets
Soft skills are interpersonal, or people, skills. They are somewhat difficult to quantify and relate to a person's personality and ability to work with others. Author Daniel Goleman's well-known book *Emotional Intelligence* discusses soft skills and their importance in the workplace. This skill set includes good communication, critical

thinking, empathy, and conflict resolution, among other skills.

Hard skills are quantifiable and teachable; they include specific knowledge and abilities required for a job. Examples of hard skills include computer programming, accounting, mathematics, and data analysis. Some can be learned on the job, while others, such as surgical skills, are first learned in a classroom and then refined through work practice.

One difference between hard skills and soft skills is that you can easily list hard skills on a resume, while soft skills may come across more clearly during an in-person job interview.

Transferable skills can apply to many different career fields. These include soft skills like critical thinking and problem solving, or hard skills such as writing and math ability.

Job-specific employment skills are those necessary for a particular position. For example, a hair stylist must know hair-coloring techniques, a payroll clerk must have payroll skills, and a nutritionist must have diet management knowledge (Doyle 4/16/18).
(https://www.thebalancecareers.com/what-is-a-skill-set-2062103)

Transferable skills deal with skills that are core to many managerial positions. For example, a top Ford manager may leave and take a job with Mattel as its CEO. It seems ludicrous that a car maker would be an effective leader of a toy manufacturer, but this proves that the skills needed for management are mostly the same in all companies. In managing people, conceptual skills, such as being able to lead and motivate people, communicate well, resolve conflicts and negotiate, take precedence over technical skills.

We talked in the previous chapter how, as a manager, you'll be looking at things differently. You'll be implementing policies and taking a different perspective as to how decisions affect your subordinates. Also, you'll be thinking in terms of the organization rather than day-to-day activities. This gives you an opportunity to perfect your "soft skills." You are now in a position where being a good communicator is key to your effectiveness and even future promotions. It's important that you empathize with subordinates to be able to lead and, in turn, have supportive followers. Also, critical thinking skills are a must for problem solving and it seems that conflict is now a part of our everyday lives, so you will need to enhance your conflict resolution skills.

Learn New Approaches
A good boss demonstrates not only key management skills, but also leadership skills. Leadership skills are more intangible and will set the good leader apart from the average leader. Good bosses have friends at work. It's a different role being in a leadership position, but good bosses are approachable, friendly, and helpful. People expect their leader to inspire, motivate, and lead by example. A good boss communicates with employees and seeks input regarding important matters. For example, fostering teamwork will boost morale and productivity. It helps the organization, but also helps employees bond with each other knowing they work in a supportive

atmosphere. Good bosses encourage teamwork and collaboration, not destructive competition. A good leader listens to subordinates and affords them opportunities to grow and progress upward in the company.

Other positive traits present in good bosses are fairness and trustworthiness. Being fair is essential to leadership and puts everyone on equal footing. Playing favorites erodes morale and will create unrest because employees know that no matter how great a job they do, it may not get them ahead or recognized. A good boss is fair all across the board and can be counted on to resolve disputes equitably. Also, trustworthiness is demonstrated by not gossiping and by holding in confidence what employees have told them on a personal level. I once had a boss that would gripe about other employees whenever I came to her office. First, it made me uneasy, and second, I wondered what she said about me to others when I left her office. A boss who is trusted commands respect, even in tough times when hard decisions have to be made. Transparency fosters trust so employees know they are not being told half-truths and they know the boss always has their best interests at heart.

Whether you're a child or the CEO of a corporation, we all need positive reinforcement. It is critical to one's success and makes us feel good about ourselves. Who doesn't appreciate words of praise or a pat on the back for a job well done? It's known that positive reinforcement and recognition are more powerful in motivating employees than money. Mark Twain, said he could live for two months on a good compliment. Positive reinforcement serves to increase productivity and improve morale individually and departmentally. It both shapes behavior and enhances an employee's self-image. It does the following *positives* for employees:

- **Enhances self-concept**. When employees feel that their efforts are being acknowledged, it leads to a sense of self-worth which helps them continue performing well. Positive reinforcement also lets the employee know he or she is making progress by doing things right. Everyone appreciates being recognized for their efforts.
- **Improves morale**. We are products of our work environment and a positive work atmosphere sets the stage for success. Happy employees are more productive and they look forward to their workday. Good morale is also a key ingredient in teamwork and to outpacing competition industrywide. An engaged employee is likely to show an interest in their work and feel motivated to do a good job.
- **Shapes positive behavior**. Rather than punishing an employee, it's more fruitful to lead them to exhibit proper behaviors by positively reinforcing expected organizational behavior when it occurs. Incentives don't always need to be monetary in nature. A meaningful reinforcement might be taking employees to lunch to celebrate the "employee of the month." Or, receiving a silver key chain for five years of no accidents can be very meaningful to employees. Everyone will strive to receive the silver key chain and it helps shape positive, productive behavior. When workers are praised or positively reinforced for good performance, it increases the likelihood that good performance will be repeated.

- **Stabilizes company culture**. When employees know they will be praised for performance if they exceed the expected standard, then it gives them reassurance. It's a stabilizing force that becomes ingrained in the company culture. Employees shouldn't be kept guessing as to whether they'll receive recognition for a job well done, they should grow to expect positive reinforcement. And, new hires will gain a sense of fitting in with the company when they're praised for their good work. The beauty of positive reinforcement and recognition is that it doesn't cost the good boss a thing and yet the investment will pay huge dividends in having happier, more satisfied and goal-oriented workers.

Power of Praise and Recognition

A study, funded by Make Their Day, an employee motivation firm, and Badgeville, a gamification company, surveyed 1,200 U.S. employees from a broad cross-section of industries. Among the study's highlights:

- 83% of respondents said recognition for contributions was more fulfilling than any rewards or
 gifts;
- 76% found peer praise very or extremely motivating;
- 88% found praise from managers very or extremely motivating;
- 90% said a "fun work environment" was very or extremely motivating.

"Workers of all ages, especially the rising Millennial population," concluded Ken Comee, Badgeville CEO, "are motivated by real-time feedback, fun, engaging work

environments, and status-based recognition over tangible rewards."
(https://www.psychologytoday.com/blog/mind-the-manager/201306/new-employee-study-shows-recognition-matters-more-money)

What about recognition and praise in the organization? How does it work? Well, besides being starved for both, employees and companies will benefit from:

- An overall positive environment in which to work
- Higher productivity
- More supportive coworkers
- More dedication and loyalty to the job and company
- Better company reputation and employees who want to stay
- Fewer accidents and better safety records

Unfortunately, the majority of us don't receive or give the amount of praise that we should. This can result in more employees being "actively disengaged" or "disengaged" in their jobs.

We hear it time and time again from research surveys that employees rate praise and recognition higher than pay or almost anything! We all want to be positively reinforced for doing a good job. The good news is that the manager will always have an unlimited budget for praise and recognition!

Balance is Key
Let's first approach work-life balance from what it is not.

Work-life balance does not mean an equal balance. Trying to schedule an equal number of hours for each of your various work and personal activities is usually unrewarding and unrealistic. Life is, and should be, more fluid than that.

Your best individual work-life balance will vary over time, often on a daily basis. The right balance for you today will probably be different for you tomorrow. The right balance for you when you are single will be different when you marry, or if you have children; when you start a new career versus when you are nearing retirement.

There is no perfect, one-size fits all, balance you should be striving for. The best work-life balance is different for each of us because we all have different priorities and different lives. (https://worklifebalance.com/work-life-balance-defined/)

In grasping the concept of work-life balance, remember that everything is best in moderation, whether it is work, diet, or exercise. The key to balancing work with your personal life is to not burnout. That's to say, you can't constantly work 12 hours a day without getting out of balance. Everyone needs a break and should take a vacation to refresh and regain perspective to realize that there's more to life than work. The old cliché, "take time to stop and smell the roses," is true. Many studies confirm that those who take vacations have a lower risk of heart disease. The human body is just not made to run continuously at high speed.

Certainly, there are times in your career when you may want to put in more hours. But when you focus too long on one thing, you lose yourself. There comes a point where stress breaks down the body and then what good is all of that overtime money?

When I started with GM, I couldn't get my work done in a 40-hour week so I began spending Saturday mornings in the office to catch up on my files, to read and study, and to plan the next week. I thought it was a great system and allowed me to produce more. I not only had to be an expert in car repairs but also at interpreting auto policies. However, of all people, our building maintenance man "ratted" me out! My manager was riding with me for a few days and when we were in the office, the maintenance man said to my boss, "I don't know what you've paying this guy, but you need to give him a raise because he even works weekends." I was appreciative of him saying that because that way the boss would be impressed with my efforts and know I was trying to be a conscientious employee. The boss asked if I was coming in on weekends and I affirmed I was. His response surprised me when he said, "don't work weekends anymore, get your job done during the week." That's all he said, and after being slightly offended, I thought "to heck with him, I was trying to show my dedication and the boss didn't even care." After more thought on my part, I realized he was right. The job was stressful and I needed the downtime on weekends. As I learned my job better and became more efficient, I eventually was able to get all work done during the week and very seldom took it home.

One problem with the preceding scenario is that even if you're voluntarily doing extra work for the company because you want to show your dedication and ambition, the time may come when you're passed over for a promotion or not recognized for all of your work. Then bitterness begins to raise its ugly head. You become resentful for working your little butt off when no one even cared or noticed. So remember the work contract: "I'll work diligently and faithfully for the company and, in turn, they will pay me and provide benefits." If you choose to put in extra time, then that is on you, not the company. Keep things in perspective and this will help keep your life in balance and burnout will not even be on the horizon.

As boss, how do you motivate your employees to do their best work? There are three relevant theories to help you understand and assist your subordinates in achieving their goals: Need Hierarchy Theory, Equity Theory, and Human Motivation Theory.

A Closer Look at Maslow's Hierarchy of Needs
Abraham Maslow first introduced his concept of a hierarchy of needs in his 1943 paper "A Theory of Human Motivation" and his subsequent book *Motivation and Personality*. This hierarchy suggests that people are motivated to fulfill basic needs before moving on to other, more advanced needs.

Maslow was interested in learning about what makes people happy and the things that they do to achieve that aim. As a humanist, Maslow believed that people have an inborn desire to be self-actualized, that is, to be all they can be. In order to achieve these ultimate goals, however, a number of more basic needs must be met such as the need for food, safety, love, and self-esteem.
There are five different levels of Maslow's hierarchy of needs. Let's take a closer look at Maslow's needs starting

at the lowest level, which are known as physiological needs.

From Basic to More Complex Needs

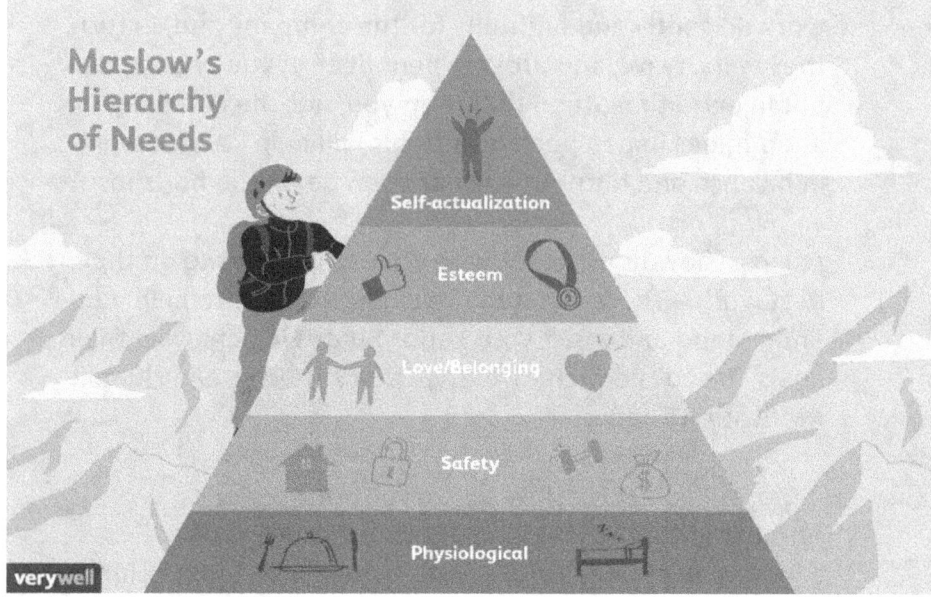

Illustration by Joshua Seong. © Verywell, 2018.

Maslow's hierarchy is most often displayed as a pyramid. The lowest levels of the pyramid are made up of the most basic needs, while the most complex needs are at the top of the pyramid.
Needs at the bottom of the pyramid are basic physical requirements including the need for food, water, sleep, and warmth. Once these lower-level needs have been met, people can move on to the next level of needs, which are for safety and security.

As people progress up the pyramid, needs become increasingly psychological and social. Soon, the need for love, friendship, and intimacy become important.

Further up the pyramid, the need for personal esteem and feelings of accomplishment take priority.

Like Carl Rogers, Maslow emphasized the importance of self-actualization, which is a process of growing and developing as a person in order to achieve individual potential.

Deficiency Needs vs. Growth Needs

Maslow believed that these needs are similar to instincts and play a major role in motivating behavior. Physiological, security, social, and esteem needs are deficiency needs, which arise due to deprivation. Satisfying these lower-level needs is important in order to avoid unpleasant feelings or consequences.

Maslow termed the highest level of the pyramid as growth needs. These needs don't stem from a lack of something, but rather from a desire to grow as a person.

While the theory is generally portrayed as a fairly rigid hierarchy, Maslow noted that the order in which these needs are fulfilled does not always follow this standard progression. For example, he noted that for some individuals, the need for self-esteem is more important than the need for love. For others, the need for creative fulfillment may supersede even the most basic needs.

Physiological Needs
The basic physiological needs are probably fairly apparent—these include the things that are vital to our survival. Some examples of the physiological needs include:
Food

Water
Breathing
Homeostasis

In addition to the basic requirements of nutrition, air and temperature regulation, the physiological needs also include such things as shelter and clothing. Maslow also included sexual reproduction in this level of the hierarchy of needs since it is essential to the survival and propagation of the species.

Security and Safety Needs
As we move up to the second level of Maslow's hierarchy of needs, the requirements start to become a bit more complex. At this level, the needs for security and safety become primary. People want control and order in their lives, so this need for safety and security contributes largely to behaviors at this level. Some of the basic security and safety needs include:
Financial security
Health and wellness
Safety against accidents and injury

Finding a job, obtaining health insurance and health care, contributing money to a savings account, and moving into a safer neighborhood are all examples of actions motivated by the security and safety needs.

Together, the safety and physiological levels of the hierarchy make up what is often referred to as the basic needs.
Social Needs
The social needs in Maslow's hierarchy include such things as love, acceptance and belonging. At this level, the need

for emotional relationships drives human behavior. Some of the things that satisfy this need include:
Friendships
Romantic attachments
Family
Social groups
Community groups
Churches and religious organizations

In order to avoid problems such as loneliness, depression, and anxiety, it is important for people to feel loved and accepted by other people. Personal relationships with friends, family, and lovers play an important role, as does involvement in other groups that might include religious groups, sports teams, book clubs, and other group activities.

Esteem Needs
At the fourth level in Maslow's hierarchy is the need for appreciation and respect. When the needs at the bottom three levels have been satisfied, the esteem needs begin to play a more prominent role in motivating behavior.

At this point, it becomes increasingly important to gain the respect and appreciation of others. People have a need to accomplish things and then have their efforts recognized.

In addition to the need for feelings of accomplishment and prestige, the esteem needs include such things as self-esteem and personal worth. People need to sense that they are valued by others and feel that they are making a contribution to the world. Participation in professional activities, academic accomplishments, athletic or team participation, and personal hobbies can all play a role in fulfilling the esteem needs.

People who are able to satisfy the esteem needs by achieving good self-esteem and the recognition of others tend to feel confident in their abilities. Those who lack self-esteem and the respect of others can develop feelings of inferiority.

Together, the esteem and social levels make up what is known as the psychological needs of the hierarchy.

Self-Actualization Needs
At the very peak of Maslow's hierarchy are the self-actualization needs. "What a man can be, he must be," Maslow explained, referring to the need people have to achieve their full potential as human beings.

According to Maslow's definition of self-actualization: "It may be loosely described as the full use and exploitation of talents, capabilities, potentialities, etc. Such people seem to be fulfilling themselves and to be doing the best that they are capable of doing... They are people who have developed or are developing to the full stature of which they are capable."

Self-actualizing people are self-aware, concerned with personal growth, less concerned with the opinions of others, and interested in fulfilling their potential (Cherry 2018).
(https://www.verywellmind.com/what-is-maslows-hierarchy-of-needs-4136760)

Application

Maslow's hierarchy of needs explains a lot about human nature and how we progress up the pyramid to satisfy our needs. But as a boss, how do you apply it? How do you use it to motivate your employees?

Let's look at hypothetical George. He's been working at the company for 10 years and, although not an outstanding employee, he is steady and a good performer. He has been a stabilizing force when helping to train new hires and is considered a "go-to" guy. But now that you are the boss of hypothetical George you want to motivate him to grow, and you can see potential in him.

While reviewing Maslow's hierarchy of needs you decide the bottom two tiers: physiological and safety/security needs have probably been satisfied. After all, hypothetical George is paid good wages and has an excellent benefit plan with the company. So then you move on up to the next tier, social and belongingness needs, and realize George has never really been a joiner. So you talk to George and ask if he'd like to join the company bowling team or be on a committee. He politely refuses the offer. So you then decide to move to the next tier, esteem needs. George hasn't been absent from work for years and you print up a certificate of recognition for him. There is an opportunity to present it to him at the next monthly department meeting with a gift card and he takes the recognition in stride. However, when George returned home that evening he couldn't wait to show his family the certificate and they were very proud of him. The upper tier, self-actualization needs, deals with growth, challenges, and learning new things, so you remind George the company has a tuition reimbursement plan if he'd like to attend some night classes at the local community college. He says he would consider it.

In summary, a good boss never stops trying to motivate subordinates to be their best. Every employee is unique and that puts the onus on the boss to determine individual motivations and assist employees in achieving, or satisfying their needs. It's not easy to be a good, effective boss and some bosses would be content to sit back, and in George's case, after the first rejection (he didn't want to be on the company bowling team) just chalk it up and never attempt to motivate George again. But you're not that kind of manager and you'll constantly look for ways to learn more about your employees in order to motivate them and help them grow. They, in turn, will reward the company by being engaged in their work through their dedication and loyalty.

Study the need hierarchy and brainstorm motivational opportunities. Maybe you see maintenance personnel wearing the same clothes all of the time, other than uniforms, or never going out for lunch because they can't afford to (physiological need). Upon further investigation, you discover they are being paid minimum wage so you lobby human resources to see about getting them more pay. Or, you could pay for their lunch once a month. Sometimes we miss opportunities right in front of us to help and motivate others.

At a company where I worked, we noticed our maintenance man would seldom smile, though he always had a good attitude. After we got to know him (always get to know your maintenance people and treat them respectfully) we found out that he needed some teeth and was ashamed to smile. So the office took up a collection to pay for his teeth and he was so grateful. He would later stop by offices, look in and smile. It was obvious that he was happy that the company cared enough to help him. From then on, we always saw him smiling and he ended up retiring with the company.

The point is, don't assume just because they're employed, that the physiological and security and safety needs are met. Those needs should be fulfilled but, then again, they may not be.

Here is a case in point about motivation and respecting individuals: We had a weight loss contest at work and there was a nominal fee to join the fun that would last eight weeks. Everyone wanted to get in shape and this was added incentive. Management appointed a person to record the contestant's weight once-a-week on Friday and the person who lost the highest percentage of weight would take home the prize money at the end of the eight weeks. Unfortunately, just a few days before the contest began, it was discovered that no females had signed up. We questioned several female employees and they all said the same thing, "My weight is no one's business and I won't reveal that to anyone." Luckily, one of my astute colleagues suggested we change it to an "honor system" contest so that people could weigh themselves using the company scales and keep track of their own weight loss. That way no one would be privy to everyone's weight and the honor system was a means of respecting individual privacy. The contest was a huge success and we later had another contest with competing teams and weekly monetary awards. The point is, don't be afraid to try new techniques to motivate people to be their best. We all like innovative thinkers and this contest was a good bonding experience. As a joke, I brought doughnuts for everyone trying to fatten them up so I could win the contest—it was obvious what I was trying to do and people accused me of sabotage, but it was all in good fun. I didn't win.

Some believe that motivation theories are a form of manipulation, and they are, if motivation theories are not used for employees' best interest. The good boss never gives up trying to motivate everyone around them. In the end, it will pay immeasurable dividends and make the company better. Sometimes it's not so easy to find out what motivates someone. In that case, simply ask what motivates them? It is certainly an acceptable question and you won't have to spend time guessing. You're not satisfied with being a good boss though. You want to be a *great* boss who listens, cares, and motivates others to achieve their goals!

Equity Theory Defined

In 1963, John Stacy Adams introduced the idea that fairness and equity are key components of a motivated individual. *Equity theory* is based on the idea that individuals are motivated by fairness, and if they identify inequities in the input or output ratios of themselves and their referent group, they will seek to adjust their input to reach their perceived equity. Adams suggested that the higher an individual's perception of equity, the more motivated they will be and vice versa: if someone perceives an unfair environment, they will be de-motivated.

The easiest way to see the equity theory at work, and probably the most common way it does impact employees, is when colleagues compare the work they do to someone else that gets paid more than them. Equity theory is at play anytime employees say things like, 'John gets paid a lot more than me, but doesn't do nearly as much work,' or 'I get paid a lot less than Jane, but this place couldn't operate without me!' In each of those situations, someone is comparing their own effort-to-compensation ratio to someone else's and is losing motivation in the process (Douglas Hawks). (https://study.com/academy/lesson/equity-theory-of-motivation-in-management-definition-examples-quiz.html)

Choices: The employees who perceive inequity and are under negative tension can make
the following choices:

- Increase inputs (I'll work harder so they'll reward me)
- Decrease inputs (I'll only exert minimal effort and someone else can pick up the slack)
- Choose a different referent (Compare with someone else)
- Quit the job
- Make demands (For instance - I know that I've performed better and harder than everyone else so I'll demand a raise)
- Rationalize (I can accept it because I really don't have the education that my coworker has)
- Do nothing and endure

Assumptions of the Equity Theory

The theory demonstrates that individuals will compare their circumstances with those of others, and that such comparisons may motivate certain kinds of behavior.

Employees will expect a fair and equitable return for their contribution to their jobs.

Perception plays a large part in comparing inputs and outcomes. If the employee perceives inequity, then they'll most likely choose from alternative actions.

Employees who perceive themselves as being in an inequitable scenario will attempt to reduce the inequity either by distorting inputs and/or outcomes psychologically, by directly altering inputs and/or outputs, or by quitting the organization.
It is important to consider equity theory factors when striving to improve an employee's job satisfaction, motivation level, etc., and what can be done to promote higher levels of each. To do this, consider the balance or imbalance that currently exists between your employee's inputs and outputs, as follows:

Inputs typically include:
*Effort
*Hard work
*Commitment
*Skill
*Flexibility
*Enthusiasm
*Trust in superiors

Outputs typically include:

*Financial rewards (such as salary, benefits, perks)
*Recognition
*Reputation
*Responsibility
*Praise
*Sense of achievement/advancement/growth
*Job security

While obviously many of these points can't be quantified and perfectly compared, the theory argues that managers should seek to find a fair balance between the inputs that an employee gives, and the outputs received. And, according to the theory, employees will be content when they perceive inputs and outputs to be in balance.

Application

Equity theory flows well with human nature because we all want to know how we're doing relative to others. It acts as a barometer for progress in one's career. Everyone wants to be treated fairly. As boss, you won't want to publish salaries. In fact, in some businesses discussing salaries can be cause for termination. However, there are critical things management can do, which include:

- Encourage questions about salaries, raises, and how the employee can progress. Discuss this in private. It lets the employee know that you are looking out for them.
- Make sure positions are properly compensated at each level in the organization and review salary ranges periodically. Keep track of any merit increases or incentives.

- If the employee perceives inequity, immediately handle their concern. Delay sends negative signals suggesting that the employee isn't important.
- Fairness goes a long way and rectifying any perceived inequity for employees will build trust because they know they can count on you to be fair.

Can You Truly Motivate Others?
We know motivation is defined as "an internal drive towards a goal," so the key word is "internal." Although there's debate over whether one can be truly motivated by another, the general consensus is that unless the person sees it for themselves (internalizes it) they won't be truly motivated. External motivation is a short-term motivator to assist the person in buying into, hopefully, long-term or internal motivation.

For example, you try to convince your child of the value of an education, but they're not sure if they want to go to college. You externally motivate by negotiating a deal with them to try college for one year at your expense and after the year is over it will be their decision whether or not they want to continue. You want the external motivation to morph into internal motivation when they see the value of a college degree and decide to pursue it for themselves. That's true motivation in action, when it's internalized.

It works the same way with employees. If they just continue to get raises sometimes it's not enough to motivate them unless they truly like their jobs. A pay raise is only an external motivator because it's short-term in nature and doesn't sustain the employee long-term.

McClelland's Human Motivation Theory

Managing a group of people with different personalities is a challenge. Human beings are complicated creatures, and their underlying motivations are just one of many complex layers that bosses must attempt to understand. It's essential to know what motivates your employees, what tasks fit them, and how they respond to praise and feedback.

The Need Theory, or Three Needs Theory, was proposed by psychologist David McClelland in the early 1960s. McClelland espoused that we all have three types of motivation regardless of age, sex, race, or culture. He says these motivators are learned, which is why his theory is sometimes also called the Learned Needs Theory. The type of motivation by which each individual is driven derives from their life experiences and their cultural environment.

According to McClelland, we are driven by three forces: need for achievement, need for affiliation, or need for power. Some of the characteristics of each motivator are listed:

MOTIVATOR	CHARACTERISTICS
	Strong need to set and accomplish challenging goals
	Prefers hierarchy with promotional positions
ACHIEVEMENT	Needs regular feedback
	Avoid low risk situations because of lack of real challenge

	Usually thrive when working alone, but can also be valued team member

MOTIVATOR	CHARACTERISTICS
	Likes group work and belonging to a team
	Needs to be loved and accepted
AFFILIATION	Prefers collaboration, not competition
	Adheres to company culture norms
	Value team membership over receiving individual praise and recognition

MOTIVATOR	CHARACTERISTICS
	Attach great value to status, recognition and reputation
	Want control
POWER	Likes to organize efforts of people
	Enjoys competition and winning
	Need to influence others

Let's take a closer look at how a boss can best manage employees using McClelland's three motivators:

Achievement
People motivated by achievement prefer working on tasks of moderate difficulty. They need challenging, but not

impossible, tasks that they can overcome or solve. High achievers can work alone, or with other high achievers. This personality type relishes setting goals and accomplishing them. When providing feedback, they like the rewards for good performance, but they also want to know what to improve upon. They can accept the good and the bad.

Affiliation
People motivated by affiliation need a group environment to thrive. They want to be liked and will conform to the group's wishes. They enjoy spending time creating and maintaining social relationships, and they have a desire to feel loved and accepted. They don't like rejection, but with their gregarious nature, they would be excellent at jobs where personal interaction is at a premium, such as customer service or sales. When management provides them with a stable work environment with little risk or uncertainty, they will excel.

Power
People motivated by a need for power want to be perceived as important and need to direct and influence others. They enjoy work and value discipline. A person motivated by power enjoys winning, whether it's arguments or contests. Competition is in their blood and they do well in goal-oriented projects or even in a negotiation for selling an idea or product. However, if their need is too great for competition and winning, they will not be open to feedback.

Application

McClelland's Need Theory, or Human Motivation Theory, states that we all have a dominant driver within the three main motivators: the needs for achievement, affiliation, or power. It's important to remember that these needs are not innate, but are learned from life experiences and our cultural environment.

Achievers like to achieve goals and accomplish tasks. Those with strong needs for affiliation value group work and social relationships. And those who are motivated by power have a strong desire to be in charge and control others. Use this information to praise, lead, and motivate your employees more effectively.

There are many motivation theories available. Read about them and apply them. I chose the Need Hierarchy Theory, Equity Theory, and Human Motivation Theory to discuss because they exemplify our work and personal lives so well. They are easy to relate to and are readily applicable.

Read Alderfer's ERG theory, Herzberg's Two-Factor theory, Vroom's Expectancy theory, Goal-Setting theory, and Reinforcement theory. Learn the theories, experiment with how to apply them and they will serve you well. Motivating your subordinates is crucial in helping them reach their potential and, in turn, making you a great boss! The workplace will be transformed into a positive atmosphere where people enjoy coming to work and facing the challenges of the day. Where they know they are treated fairly and they can trust and look up to their boss.

Summary

In summary, to become a great boss, start with improving your skill set. Work on interpersonal, communication, critical thinking, and conflict resolution skills. Show that you are trustworthy and fair when dealing with others. Communicate, don't dictate!

It is important to dedicate yourself to the new position of manager, but remember a stressed, burned out boss is of no use to anyone. So try to keep things in balance and try not to sacrifice too much of your personal life and family time for the sake of the company. You'll actually be a better boss because you'll have a healthy perspective when tackling organizational issues.

Immerse yourself in motivation theories. Chew on them, swallow them, and digest them. You don't have to be a psychologist, but knowing your employees and some basic elements of motivation will help get the most out of them. They will be happier, fulfilled employees and that adds to efficiency. You will be happier and fulfilled also, because it will prevent many problems in the workplace. Don't be afraid to try new motivational techniques. Maybe some won't work, but most will. Figure out the best ways to motivate your employees. That's the optimum way to grow because you want to progress beyond the attitude of "they're just working for a paycheck." Using motivation strategies will help the company in so many ways that include helping the company prosper; helping subordinates achieve satisfaction, and helping you achieve self-satisfaction for being a good boss who is respected and well-liked.

3. Where Does Your Power Come From?

Sure, the boss has the power to fire us, just as we have the power to quit. But where does all of that power come from and what separates a manager from a leader or are they one and the same? As a *manager*, you will have three types of power conveyed upon you by the organization, and as a *leader* you may have two types of power. Hopefully, an effective manager is also an effective leader, but this is not always the case. Sad to say, you can be one without the other.

Sources of Power

In 1959, social psychologists John R.P. French and Bertram H. Raven identified five sources, or forms of power, from which a person gets power. These sources are now known as *French and Raven's Five Bases of Power*. They are briefly explained as follows:

1. **Legitimate Power**-also known as position power and official power. It comes from the higher authority in an organization; a manager gets power because of his or her position or post. It gives them the power to control resources and to reward and punish others. For example, a chief executive officer (CEO) of a company gets legitimate powers because of the position she or he holds. Also, it's important that for positional power to be exercised effectively, subordinates must know it was earned legitimately.
2. **Coercive Power**-is the ability to punish others or to pose a threat to others. Coercive power uses fear as a motivator. The leaders or managers with coercive powers can threaten an employee's job security, cut their pay, withdraw certain facilities, suspend them, etc. Coercive power helps control the behavior of employees by ensuring that they adhere to the organization's policies and norms. Though coercive power may have an impact in the short-run; it may create a negative impact on the receiver.
3. **Reward Power**-is the opposite of coercive power. With the help of reward power the manager tries to motivate the followers to improve their performance. This power enables the leader to recognize the services of subordinates through appreciation. However, if it's applied through favoritism, reward power can greatly demoralize employees and diminish their output.
4. **Referent Power**-also known as personal power, charismatic power, and the power of personality. This power comes from each leader individually

and derives from the interpersonal relationships that a person cultivates with other people in the organization. It is the personality of the person that attracts followers. People follow because they are influenced or attracted by the magnetic personality of the leader. The followers admire their leaders and may even try to copy their behavior, dress, etc. John F. Kennedy, Martin Luther King, and Mahatma Gandhi are examples of leaders with referent power.
5. **Expert Power**-also known as the power of knowledge. It comes from expert knowledge and skills. Expert power means the expert influences another person's behavior. This is because the expert has knowledge and skill which the other person needs but does not possess. Such people are highly valued by organizations for their problem solving skills. People like doctors, lawyers, accountants, etc., have expert power because they have knowledge and skills which others require. Possession of expert power is normally a stepping stone to other sources of power such as legitimate power. For example, a person who holds expert power can be promoted to senior management, thereby giving them legitimate power (http://kalyan-city.blogspot.com/2011/08/five-bases-of-power-by-john-french-and.html).

Management vs Leadership
Can one be a manager without being a leader or a leader without being a manager? Of course! An effective manager should be viewed as both. What are some of the differences between a manager and a leader? Well, we know the manager already has three of the five bases of

power bestowed on them from the organization: legitimate, coercive, and reward. It's a no-brainer that those three are built into the position. The challenge for the boss is acquiring the other two bases of power: expert and referent. Expert power may not necessarily be needed in a management position because of losing some expertise moving through the levels from subordinate to manager. Due to the nature of being in management your high technical skills may be slowly replaced with conceptual skills in order to motivate employees, interpret policies, and direct subordinates.

So, while they might sound similar, a "boss" and a "leader" have slightly different meanings. When you are boss (manager) it means that you are in charge of a team or the whole organization. A boss is supposed to assign tasks, have control over employees and make crucial decisions.

Here is a list of traits that make up a *strong manager*, some of the key characteristics are:

- Ability to direct day-to-day work efforts.
- Process management: establish work rules, standard and operating procedures.
- People focused: look after people, their needs, listen to them and involve them.
- Relies on control: people know the consequences if they get out of line.

(https://www.go2hr.ca/management-leadership/understanding-the-differences-leadership-vs...)

Here is a list of traits that make up a *strong leader*, some of the key characteristics are:

- Sells: has great ideas and persuades people to join in.
- Challenges status quo: "I know it isn't broken, but is there a way to do it even better?"
- Thinks long-term: "Let's look beyond the cost today and explore what this investment can mean down the road."
- Inspires trust: honesty and integrity are standard and workers know they are trusted.

(https://www.resourcefulmanager.com/leaders-vs-managers/)

Summary

In summary, as a boss, you have three bona fide sources of power: legitimate, coercive, and reward. We know these are conveyed on the position by the organization. However, more importantly, you need to acquire referent and expert power to elevate yourself to being a great boss! Do employees look up to you? Do they communicate readily? Do they tell you their goals and ambitions? Can they confide in you? Is your door always open to employees? Do you support their efforts? Strive to be a manager *and* a leader, and you will be a tremendous asset to the company for as long as you choose to work there.

4. Poor Bosses. We've All Had Them.

<u>Human Relations is at the Heart of Everything</u>
I have been teaching human relations classes for over 30 years and I can testify to the fact that human relations is at the heart of everything we do. From the restaurant wait staff, to the way you interact with family, to how you get along at work, it all revolves around interacting with our fellow human beings because we are social animals.
When you interact with other people, are they positive or negative interactions?

I can't count the times students have said to me, "I wish my boss would take this human relations class." It's unfortunate that we've lost common courtesies because of the speed of technology and people always striving to get ahead. Many times it's at the expense of others but we're oblivious to it. People who are continuously plugged into technology oftentimes don't mean to be rude, but they are. When you're driving, or in the store, or at the doctor's office, or at the bank, or even in a restaurant, how many people are on their cellphones? I observed a mother and daughter recently at a restaurant. They were sitting across from each other and they were both on their cellphones. I never noticed them even talking to each other. Hopefully they were texting one another?

Technology has sped up our lives and we expect things to be done instantaneously. It's evident in the workplace when the boss calls you at home. There is no place to escape from your workday and people even take their laptops and work on their vacations. Bad bosses tap into the belief that you are there for them every hour of every day and it stresses employees.

Everyone wants a workplace where they are free to interact, their opinions make a difference, where they are trusted and the boss combines great leadership with managing duties. In short, we want to respect and trust our boss.

Signs You Have a Terrible Boss
National Bosses Day, which is celebrated in the U.S. on October 16 each year, is a day for employees to show appreciation for their managers. But if you have a nightmare of a boss, you probably have little to thank them for this year. As it turns out, a terrible boss doesn't

just impact the way you work in the office. It affects your entire life.

Merideth Ferguson, assistant professor of management at Utah State University and coauthor of a study conducted by Baylor University, calls this the "spillover effect," meaning your work life also affects your marriage and other intimate relationships.

According to another survey commissioned by Lynn Taylor Consulting, a whopping 19.2 hours are wasted each week worrying about what a boss says or does – 13 of which occur during the workweek, and 6.2 over the weekend. That's more than 2 hours every workday that you worry about the boss!

"A bad boss will likely jeopardize your career growth and impact your personal life," Lynn Taylor explains. "A good manager will help you thrive and bring out the best in you. While it's rarely at the top of your mind, you can empower yourself with a terrible boss, especially if you watch for red flags."

It's important to identify these signs early on, before you get too involved, especially if you spot them during the job interview. This way, you can decide if it's something you actually want to deal with (or you can figure out if you'll need to start looking for a new job).

Here are some signs your boss will eventually crush all happiness you're clinging to – and steps you can take along the way:

1. **Your boss is never, ever wrong**. Learning to admit that you're wrong is one of the best things you can do for your colleagues. If your boss refuses to admit that they're wrong, this means they're not willing to go out of their comfort zone for you. A national independent study by Lynn Taylor Consulting found that 91% of employees said that owning up to one's mistakes as a manager was an important factor in employee job satisfaction. "Admitting to mistakes sends a message to your employees that it's a safe environment to take smart risks – and without that, your sapping innovation," Taylor says.
2. **Your boss over promises**. An over-promising boss is an untrustworthy boss. "You might have been promised a series of promotions, increased responsibility, or a raise, but all you get is silence," says Taylor. "It's often helpful to get to the truth through emails, if one-on-one discussions are getting you nowhere. If the responses aren't coming via email, or at all, be wary."
3. **They have a pesky habit of calling you on your day off**. You put in your hours and get permission for a long weekend off, but your boss doesn't hesitate to call you during your off hours. To deal with this kind of boss, you need to set your boundaries early. "'Separation anxiety' can kick in if you have a power-hungry boss, and you inadvertently chip away at that power," adds Taylor. "You're best served to instill a sense of comfort with a terrible boss who's demanding, much as you would with a 'terrible two' toddler – whether you plan to take a day off, leave early, arrive late, or take vacation." If you're going to be gone, give ample warning and

let them know that things are under control, with appropriate detail.

4. **Your boss is a micro-manager.** Is your boss so pushy and overbearing that you find yourself unable to accomplish anything efficiently? This may be a perpetual problem, so get ready for it early. If they want a play-by-play of every meeting, email, and call, then take detailed notes of every business interaction and send them to your boss. Your boss will think that they're on top of things and will leave your alone. "By over-communicating with a micro-manager or needy boss, you'll diffuse their desire to constantly check in, while you build all-important trust at the same time," says Taylor.

5. **Your boss has favorites.** This will cloud their ability to recognize your skills and the value you add to the company. They also fail to see that they're treating you unfairly. "No matter how hard you work, or the results you achieve, they somehow become dwarfed by those of the teacher's pet," Taylor explains. "It's worth modeling good behavior in this scenario, praising others on your staff or those in other departments, for their *team* effort. You're giving recognition to those who deserve it and demonstrating the powerful impact that has for people like you."

6. **They're passive aggressive or ignore you.** One of the most unnerving, tell-tale signs of a terrible boss is one who rarely lets you know where you (or they) stand. "Most employees would rather get direct criticism from their manager than face a seemingly pleasant, but backstabbing boss," Taylor explains. If they're simply not attentive, that's also a problem. "When your boss has the attention

span of a fly, it not only saps your motivation; you feel like you're spinning your wheels," she says. "Try observing how others get the manager's attention."

7. **They're quick to blame you for mistakes, but rarely express gratitude when you succeed.** Does your boss put you down in front of others? If you let it go once, it'll happen over and over again. Good bosses know they should have this conversation with their employees in private.

8. **It's getting harder for you to wake up in the morning.** If you have a knot in your gut every time you have to face your boss, or if it's taking you twice as long to drag yourself out of bed every morning, take notice. You may just have a terrible boss. "The worst thing you can do is nothing," says Taylor. "Better to first examine if this is a relationship worth salvaging with some diplomatic, high-road tactics."

9. **Your boss never discusses your future with you.** Are the discussions with your manager mostly transactional, with rare discussions about your future growth path? A good boss will discuss your prospects for long-term growth within the company – and not just during your performance evaluation, Taylor explains. "Savvy bosses check in with their team on a regular basis, rather than being reactive or waiting for an emergency, such as your brand new job offer."

10. **Your boss throws tantrums easily.** No one should be subjected to an out-of-control boss. "If you have been, your next step might be to check out your favorite job board," says Taylor. But if your manager only has occasional outbursts, you may be

able to work through the situation. "Timing is important with emotionally prone bosses; don't go into the lion's den in your zeal for approvals, and certainly avoid early mornings, just before lunch, or after some bad company news."

11. **Your work is never enough**. "It's 8:30 a.m. and your inbox is crashing the corporate server due to your boss' excessive requests and inquiries," says Taylor. "You could work 24/7 and still find your boss dissatisfied." Your manager must realize that you have limited time in a day, and can't do all things (well) at once. If you don't speak up, your boss will keep pushing. (Jacquelyn Smith 10/15/14) (https://www.businessinsider.com/signs-you-have-a-terrible-boss-2014-10?op=1)

Here are some additional signs you have a bad boss:

- **Being too hands-off (not enough direction)**
  Does your boss know what you're working on, what challenges you're facing, and what you need in order to succeed? It's possible we're yearning for leadership, recognition, and guidance – things we might seek elsewhere if the boss doesn't provide them.
- **Being authoritative and/or insensitive**
  When it's time to make a decision, does the boss seek input from employees or just hand down a decree that suits their own narrative of what you need? The boss may be smart, and may even be right most of the time, but if he or she isn't seeking input (or disregarding the input received), they might come across as uncaring or authoritative –

pretty undesirable traits in any organization aside from a dictatorship.

- **Being too democratic/sensitive/indecisive**
On the other hand, if the boss can't make a decision without consulting with everyone, or if they take forever to provide a ruling because they're worried about stepping on toes or making a mistake, then they are not doing enough leading. People want to look up to their leaders for direction and reassurance. If the boss can't take the reins, the wagon is bound to run off the road.

- **Being hypocritical/inconsistent**
What's worse than being authoritarian or indecisive? Combining the two in an unpredictable way: saying or doing one thing, then contradicting yourself with hypocritical actions or decisions down the road. That's not to say the boss should be inflexible or rigid; it just means that if people can't rely on management to be consistent, they won't be able to trust their leadership when it really matters.

- **Treating everyone alike**
We don't treat every one of our friends and family the same way, and while employees aren't as close as family, they, too, deserve individual treatment. How does the boss act when he or she speaks with introverts on your team, compared with the extroverts? Do they consider things like an employee's personal space, sense of humor, hot buttons, and reward centers? If the boss doesn't, they probably have a decent relationship with some employees, the ones who fit the communication mold they use, and a big

communication gap with the other employees (Rob de Luca 5/23/2018).
(https://www.bamboohr.com/blog/11-poor-management-offenses-you-may-not-know-your...)

Your Bad Boss May Be Unaware He or She Is Bad
Start your campaign by understanding that your boss may not know that she is a bad boss. Just as in situational leadership, the definition of **bad** depends on the employee's needs, the manager's skills and the circumstances.

A hands-off manager may not realize that her failure to provide any direction or feedback makes her a bad boss. She may think she's *empowering* her staff. A manager who provides too much direction and micromanages may feel insecure and uncertain about her own job. She may not realize her direction is insulting to a competent, secure, self-directed staff member.
Or, maybe the boss lacks training and is so overwhelmed with his job requirements that he can't provide support for you.

Perhaps he has been promoted too quickly, or his reporting responsibilities have expanded beyond his reach. In these days of downsizing, responsibilities are often shared by fewer staff members than ever before, which can affect their ability to do the job well.

This bad boss may not share your values.

The youngest generations of workers expect that they can use their vacation time and take action to make work-life balance a priority. A flexible work schedule may make the job their dream job. But, not all bosses share these views. Some, for example, think that remote workers harm the culture and interfere with developing a culture of teamwork.

If your values are out of sync with those of your boss, and you don't think this imbalance will change, you do have a problem. Maybe it's time to change bosses. But, until then, these actions are recommended for you to preserve your relationship, such as it is.

    Recommended Approach to the Unwitting Bad Boss Talk to this boss. Tell him what you need from him in terms of direction, feedback, and support. Be polite and focus on your needs. You need to tell the boss exactly what you need from him. Telling the boss that he's a bad boss is counterproductive and won't help you meet your goals.

Ask the manager how you can help him reach his goals. Make sure you listen well and provide the needed assistance he requests.

Seek a mentor from among other managers or more skilled peers, with the full knowledge and cooperation of your current manager, to enlarge your opportunity for experience.

If you've taken these actions, and they haven't worked, go to your boss's manager and ask for assistance. Or, you can go to your Human Resources staff first, to rehearse and gain advice. Understand that your current boss may never forgive you, so ensure that you have done what you can do with him, before taking your issues up the line.

You may never hear what the boss's boss or the HR staff did to help solve your bad manager's behavior. It's confidential. But, do allow some time to pass for the actions to have their desired impact.

If nothing changes, despite your best efforts, and you think the problem is that they don't believe you, draw together coworkers who also experience the behavior. Visit the boss's manager to help him see the size and impact of the behavior.

If you think the problem is that your boss can't— or won't—change, ask for a transfer to another department. This recommendation presumes you like your employer and your work, so you don't regard quitting or job searching as your best option.

If a transfer or promotion is unavailable, begin your search for a new job. Fleeing is always an option. You may want to conduct your job search secretly, but under the circumstances, it may be time for you to go.

When the Bad Boss Knows

A manager at a mid-sized manufacturing company wanted to improve his approach to working with his employees. He knew that he looked down his nose at them. He criticized and screamed at employees. He publicly humiliated any employee who made a mistake, as examples.

One day he called to ask a question of his consultant. The question doomed him to disappointment when he said, "I know that you don't approve of me screaming at staff as a regular thing." Agreed, he then said. "So, can you tell me, please, what are the circumstances under which it is okay for me to scream at them?"

This manager thought his behavior was perfectly acceptable. (The end of the story? He never did change and was eventually removed as manager.) Most managers that bully, intimidate, cruelly criticize, name-call and treat you as if you are stupid likely know what they are doing. They may know they're bad and even revel in their badness.

They may feel their behavior has been condoned—and even encouraged—within their organization. They may have learned the behaviors from their former supervisor who was viewed as successful.

You don't have to put up with demeaning behavior. You deserve a good boss who helps your self-confidence and self-esteem grow. You deserve a good boss who helps you advance your career. You deserve civil, professional treatment at work.

Recommended Approach to the Bad Boss Who Knows He's Bad

Start by recognizing that you have the right to a professional environment in your workplace. You are not the problem. You have a bad boss. He is the problem. You need to deal with him.

You can try talking with the bad boss to tell him the impact that his actions or words are having on you or your performance. In a rare blue moon, the bad boss might care enough to work to modify his behavior.

If he does decide to work on his behavior, hold him to his

commitments. If you allow him to yell at you, even just a little bit, you are training him that he can get away with his former behavior. Don't go to war publicly, but draw his behavior to his attention as soon as you have the opportunity, privately.

If the behavior does not change, appeal to his supervisor and to Human Resources staff. Describe exactly what he does and the impact the behavior is having on you and your job performance.

Again, you may never hear what the boss's boss or the HR staff did to help solve your bad manager's behavior. It's confidential. But, do allow some time to pass for the actions they may have tried to have their desired impact.

If nothing changes, despite your best efforts, and you think the problem is that they don't believe you, draw together coworkers who also experience the behavior. Visit the boss's manager to help him see the size and impact of the behavior.

If you think the problem is that your boss can't—or won't—change, ask for a transfer to another department. This recommendation presumes that you like your employer and your work. If not, job searching may be your next best option.

If a transfer or promotion is unavailable, begin your search for a new job for sure. Fleeing is always an option if your bad boss won't change. You may want to conduct your job search secretly, but under the circumstances, it may be time for you to go. (Susan M. Heathfield, 6/10/2018)

(https://www.thebalancecareers.com/bad-to-the-bone-dealing-with-a-bad-boss-1917714)

Bad Bosses Infect the Workplace
- **Fear**. Managing through fear is like a dictatorial parent who says, "I always know what's best, don't you dare question me!" That may work at home but it's not a healthy relationship at work when you are ruled by fear. There is no interaction and communication is always one-way, that is, top-down. "I'm the experienced boss and you're the subordinate, so listen and learn." This kind of leadership never gives the employee chances for input and demeans them.
- **Company reputation**. Everything a manager says and does is a reflection on the company. If poor management is pervasive throughout the organization, word gets around and the company's image will be tarnished. With social media being so popular, people will learn of horror stories at the company and not want to work there. How does management talk about competitors? If they constantly run down their competition, it reflects negatively on the organization. This is also a sign of poor communication.
- **Mental/physical**. We know that stress sends many Americans to the doctor. Living and working are stressful enough without adding a bad boss onto our stress mountain. Not only are we spending billions on doctor's and medication, but we're setting ourselves up for chronic illness. It's well-documented that continued stress on the body manifests itself in lowering the immune system. A

weak immune system cannot fight off viruses and may be the cause of serious illness, even cancer.

- **Lack of training**. "Directing and controlling" have given way to "coaching and training." If the organization is to succeed, it starts with properly trained employees, including managers. Playing favorites and promoting an unqualified employee into management will wreak havoc with his or her subordinates. There will be constant morale and turnover issues because employees are living in an arbitrary atmosphere where hard work and qualifications don't necessarily pay off. They have no stability.
- **High turnover**. Who wants to continue working for a bad boss? A manager who doesn't perform their job duties properly infects the organization. Poor communications, authoritative commands, lack of good decision making, and micro-managing are just a few ways to run people off. Employees learn quickly if the organization and management cares about them. Is the new hire properly oriented and trained to have the tools to succeed? Is there a positive team atmosphere in the workplace? People quit their jobs for all sorts of reasons, but the majority quit *the boss*, not the company.
- **Role model**. Management must lead by example. The "do as I say," not "as I do," leadership mantra is not sending positive messages to employees. It is telling them that it's acceptable to take shortcuts and not follow company guidelines. A dangerous precedent is set when bosses bend rules and use a double-standard to view their employees. The more managers stray, the more employees will stray.

- **No motivation or positive reinforcement.** Yes, employees work for a paycheck, but they work for much more than that. Survey after survey, employees rate "appreciation," "recognition," and "sense of accomplishment," higher than pay. Work is a form of expression, receiving a paycheck and being allowed to return the next week is not motivation. We are social beings who need positive reinforcement when a job is done well. If the boss doesn't recognize good work, it sends signals to subordinates that their work doesn't matter. Soon, work will be done to minimum standards with nothing extra added. Without motivation and positive reinforcement, employees begin not to care about their work and will look for employment where they are valued.

An American Tragedy

Roughly 25 to 30 percent of our lives will be spent at work! It's actually much more than that because when we are not working, we are thinking about work. This emphasizes the importance of having a good boss even more. Work gives us a purpose and it is true that when we are not happy at work, we actually quit the boss, not the company. A poor boss overshadows everything!
Think of all of the sorry bosses you've had in your life. There are probably more bad than good. See if you can relate to the following:

1. **Re-apply for your job.** We were moving to a new branch and one boss came up with the brilliant idea of making people re-apply for their jobs! It was the most ridiculous thing most of us had ever heard of and she,

evidently, had the blessing of upper management. It seemed a coward's way out to just not re-hire someone rather than stepping up and telling them they were not performing and they would be let go. This manager actually told one staff member, whose husband was critically ill at the time and died a few weeks later, that she might have to take a cut in pay if she were re-hired. The employee was an excellent, conscientious worker and it was incredibly insensitive to treat her that way. In fact, the office was in such an uproar that the manager backed down and finally agreed that the staff member's job was safe.

2. **Immaturity**. A friend was so sure that he would get to be dean at the college after he applied for the position, that he started telling everyone what he would do when he got the job. We cautioned him that there were other applicants and he should wait to see if he'd get the promotion. However, he wasn't listening to any of us and just continued to believe that he was the future dean. Well, he didn't get the position and he pouted throughout the semester until he finally quit and went to another college. He had lost face and was embarrassed. It was very immature behavior on his part, but our warnings to him fell on deaf ears.

3. **The all-powerful**. I had been an adjuster for four months with General Motors and, being grateful for the opportunity, I took pride in my work. There was a big learning

curve, but I was bright-eyed and enthusiastic having my first full-time job fresh out of college at age 21. The scenario was developing that I had too many claims to handle and advice from my mentor always helped. While I was trying to juggle my time to give good service to everyone I received an engine fire claim. My mentor told me to call the dealership and let them get started on repairs, then drop by in a few days and finish up the claim. Well, I never got by the dealer because of my claim load, but it seemed like a minor claim anyway. After talking with the service department, they said they had replaced the wiring harness, painted the hood, and were basically through with repairs. Unfortunately, when they added water to the radiator it leaked through to the oil pan, which meant it probably had a cracked engine block and the claimant was making a fraudulent claim trying to get a new engine. He had obviously set the fire on purpose and after investigating and inspecting the crack in the block, I denied the claim. But we still had to pay the dealer for the repairs they'd done. I called the claim manager in El Paso, apologized, and gave an explanation. He seemed to accept that I'd made an error and that I'd learned from it. Well, lo and behold, my immediate claim supervisor came to visit the following week. I was five minutes late to his motel room because he'd given me the wrong room number but he chewed on me about promptness when I arrived. He then proceeded to chew on me for over an hour over things I'd done wrong. At one point, I excused myself and had to walk outside to cool down. I also called my fiancé and told her we might have to postpone the wedding because I was going to tell the supervisor what he could do with this job! My fiancé backed me fully. When I returned to the room, I was totally disheartened and even asked him if he could tell me anything positive, like my shoelaces were tied right (I was wearing loafers). He then said, "I only have time to tell you the things you're doing wrong." After the visit was over, I had lost respect for the supervisor and called the claim manager. I told him that I was prepared to resign if he felt I couldn't do the job to GM's satisfaction. And he basically said that I was doing a good job and to not let this get me down. I worked there for 13 years and had many more bad managers than good. It was apparent to me early on that I would not retire with that organization.

4. **It's all relative**. I worked at an institution where nepotism ran rampant and one boss was put in a position of authority that was not qualified for the position, but he had a relative in administration so he got the job. He neither had the experience nor the education to be in that position. Many faculty members had no respect for him but

had to adhere to his decisions because he was boss. There were instances where I would specifically do things to make him do his job, but at one point he told me not to email him anymore. He said to just call him if I had a problem. He once made wholesale changes to a program that simply needed tweaking to help increase enrollment, but enrollment went down with his new program. He went so far as to change the program name, which confused students, and even changed courses, which made it very difficult for teachers. The teachers had new courses and new textbooks to prepare from in a matter of weeks. They were extremely anxious about all of the changes, and rightly so. He never asked the teachers in the program for their input and simply made a unilateral decision, much to the dismay of many of the faculty. It was a case of not listening and not caring about your subordinates because he always knew best. Morale suffered for many and overhauling the entire program was unnecessary. What a shame!

Along that same vein, we had a wife supervising another family member, who just happened to be her husband; a clear violation found on any organization chart. Our own policy and procedure manual actually forbade this, but upper management must not have read their own manual. When management bends and breaks rules for no apparent reason, employees no longer trust and wonder if hard work actually pays off. Everyone walks around in disbelief with low morale being the price paid.

5. **One boss and one spy**. We had an employee whose immediate boss was located at another branch a few miles away. Unfortunately, this employee worked with a very good friend of her immediate boss, so everything this employee said and did was relayed to her boss through the "spy" (friend). This was not only a breach of the "one employee, one boss," rule, but it was also unethical. The friend of the boss reported if the employee was late to work or any gossip on hand. It lowered office morale considerably and after nothing was done, the employee quit. No one should have a "snitch" watching over their shoulder throughout the workday. Before it came to the point of the employee leaving, the boss should have been mature enough to tell her "friend" not to make any more reports on the coworker because it was really none of her business. But, it never happened and a good employee was lost due to poor management.

6. **Do nothing boss**. I worked in an office where the boss was totally laid back, and I mean so laid back that he very seldom made a decision or enforced rules. We had a dress code and a coworker, Dennis, would constantly come to work in torn jeans, a lumberjack shirt, and torn cap. This sent a

very bad message to customers and our dress code only stated to dress "professionally." I confronted Dennis one day and he just laughed it off. It was not my job to do that and we were equals in the office, but several of us had said something to the boss and there was never a change. The result was having employees with low morale because they saw the boss take no action to correct the situation. We decided to continue to dress professionally, do our jobs, and not confront Dennis anymore. We had no power to resolve the problem. Unfortunately, we lost respect for the boss.

7. **The Rigid Boss.** One boss had rules such as: You will smile at all times, spend no more than 10 minutes per client--there are others waiting, morning tardiness will be taken out of your paycheck, you will punch the time clock every morning, at break, at lunch, upon leaving, and so on. It was a stifling atmosphere and there was no way to limit each client to 10 minutes. That would be rude because some people needed more time than others. I knew a lady that tended to chat with clients and it would upset the boss, but she brought in more business than anyone in the office and the boss couldn't see that. After the employee left the company, some clients moved their business elsewhere since they had lost their "go-to" person.

What To Do When You Have a Bad Boss

The problems we face when we have a bad boss are almost too numerous to mention, but the two biggest issues are:

1. They can negatively impact our work performance.
2. They can make life miserable.

These two issues alone make it worth trying to figure out how to work more effectively with our boss, even when they are bad.

There is a catch-all term we use regarding bosses and co-workers called "being difficult." It's not too specific to exactly know what the issue is. Sometimes, when we are in the midst of a constant barrage from the bad boss, it's hard to know exactly where the difficulty may lie. All we know is it is difficult to work successfully with this person. Here are some suggestions that might help reduce the level of difficulty:

> 1. **Look to your own performance first**. You might think they are being difficult, because they are demanding a different level of output from you. Make sure you are clear on what they expect from you.
> 2. **Realize you may have opposing styles**. You might be expecting something from your boss that they simply can't do. You might think they are unfriendly simply because they fail to say "Good Morning." To them, that might simply be a waste of time. Examine your own expectations of what you think they should be doing. They may not be very outgoing or

simply operate differently than what you're used to. Reset your expectations. (Side note: I tend to be light-hearted and try not to take things too seriously. Finally, after a few months I realized that my boss had no sense of humor and our personalities clashed. I learned when dealing with the boss to never joke or use humor and get down to business quickly. Though we still have disagreements, the relationship is a working relationship and I don't ever use humor around him).

3. **Learn the boss**. Spend some time really observing this person to see what they do that is impacting you. In the process, you might learn that they are getting leaned on by their boss and it's creating extra stress. You could discover they aren't a morning person, meaning you should delay important interactions until after lunch. Figure out their rhythms and modify your own.

4. **Don't shrink**. All too often, when we don't like someone, we go out of our way to avoid them. While this tactic can work to keep you under the radar, wait to do that until you clearly have exhausted all your options. You may also find that more, not less, communication can help you with this type of person. Shrinking away into a dark corner won't help you.

5. **Become indispensable**. If you've attempted to learn more about the boss, take it to the next level of problem solving and support. This will help you shine to your own boss and will reduce reasons for finding fault

with you. You could become the "go-to" person that they respect and depend on.

6. **Let it roll off of you**. We will spend a lifetime of running into people that are demanding, critical, and downright volatile. You need to learn the skill of blowing most of it off. Certainly, there will be some of it that will still bother you, but most of the time you simply try to not let it penetrate. That's not to suggest ignoring the boss's demands, but keeping it in perspective and looking at the big picture can help you deal with it. (https://www.workitdaily.com/what-do-have-bad-boss/)

The Power of Expectations

Aren't expectations a drag when they're not met? Isn't it a shame that we don't expect good service anymore? And when we do receive good service, since it's rare, we write the person's name down and remember to do business with them again. Whether it's a restaurant, a work organization, or your spouse, we all have expectations that shouldn't be ignored.

What about your work expectations? You probably expect all of the following:

- Consistent rules and policies
- Dependable co-workers
- Fair management
- Safe work environment
- Timely training
- Challenging, enjoyable work
- A full day's work for a full day's pay

- Qualified managers and leaders
- Stable organization
- Good pay
- Timely communication from management and to be listened to
- Recognition and appreciation

These are simply common workplace expectations. Many expectations are learned when hired, through orientation. They tell us what we can and cannot do in the organization. We are told our job responsibilities so we know our duties in the organization. It's their expectations of us. These are critical if the company is to be efficient and remain competitive in the industry. So the company trains us and we know what to expect, but what about the expectations we have of the boss? We have a right to expect them to be fair, to be good role models, to keep us apprised of company developments, to give us a raise as soon as is practicable, and to make needed training available to keep skills refreshed. Develop the type of relationship where you can talk to your boss about expectations. Tell the bad boss what you expect of him or her. Maybe they'll get the message, and you'll have aired your expectations which will send your boss the message that you want to continue working there, if some things change. If you fear reprisal, or they won't listen, then find another job where you can communicate well with management! There are poor bosses out there who are not qualified or are on a power trip and unless the company realizes it and corrects it, things will never change. Hey, you'll be working for 40+ years, find a job where you'll be happy!

The **Pygmalion effect** states that we tend to live up to *others'* expectations. Research results show a positive correlation between leader expectations and follower performance. It seems intuitive that we would desire to live up to a leader's expectations of us. When you believe in your subordinates, you'll get the most out of them.

The Pygmalion effect works because we don't want to let people down and we will try hard to achieve what they believe we can achieve. However, expectations must be prefaced with realism. If you constantly expect too much and the employee continually falls short, then you're killing their desire to please you and achieve the goal. They will throw in the towel thinking, "I can never meet those expectations, so why even try."

While mostly positive, the effect could have a negative influence if the pressure is too great to perform well. For example, often parents expect straight "A's" from junior. Yet, if the son or daughter is giving their best effort and still falling short of expectations, it could result in added stress. The negative effects would be not trying hard and grades going down because they know they can never meet their parents' expectations.

Expectations work both ways, whether relating to teachers and students, or bosses and employees. Suppose you've told your boss the expectations you have for them and they're not listening, or you were afraid to sit down and confront your boss with the expectations you have. Okay, one more approach is to dig deep and see if you can tell if your boss is a Theory X manager (covered in Chapter 6). He or she may be viewing you that way because they don't trust you and they have little hope of you being a good employee. If you've come to that conclusion, then try proving the boss wrong and make them a better boss in the process. Try not complaining, doing your work in a timely manner, doing quality work, and being a dependable go-to employee. It may change the way the boss views you and, in turn, make for a better boss.

Summary

In summary, it's easy for employees to bash the boss. After all, he or she is to blame for everything that goes wrong or that you disagree with. And to a large extent, that's true. We know bad bosses make our lives miserable. They create frustration and stress in our lives which carries over to lives outside of work. We are having more arguments with the spouse, the kids are misbehaving, the dog chewed up your slippers, and the crazy neighbor won't turn down the music.

Before you tell the bad boss off and quit, step back and think of why you accepted employment with this particular company. Did it look like the kind of work you'd enjoy? Were coworkers friendly and supportive? Had you always looked up to the company and wanted to someday work there? Did you feel you could make a difference in the world with this kind of work?

If so, then try to empathize with the bad boss. You have nothing to lose at this point and it may shed some light on your relationship. Is the boss going through major life events, such as: divorce, separation, death of a loved one, kids in trouble with the law? Is the boss fairly new to the position? Does he or she lack training? Are they related to someone in the company? (i.e., the CEO's son) Do you see the possibility that the boss will change for the better?

Sometimes it's helpful to be grateful for what you have. During the recession of 2007-2009, there were many people laid off and who couldn't find work. I was working in a less than stellar job, but I was grateful to be employed so I put my head down and trudged on. Along with analyzing your work situation be sure to also list the good things about it.

Take everything into consideration and if you decide to stick it out, then try to talk to the boss, readjust your attitude, or offer to help in some way. You've got to break down the barriers and tell them your expectations of them, and about your own goals. It is tough to supervise or work with complex human beings, and we are all complex.

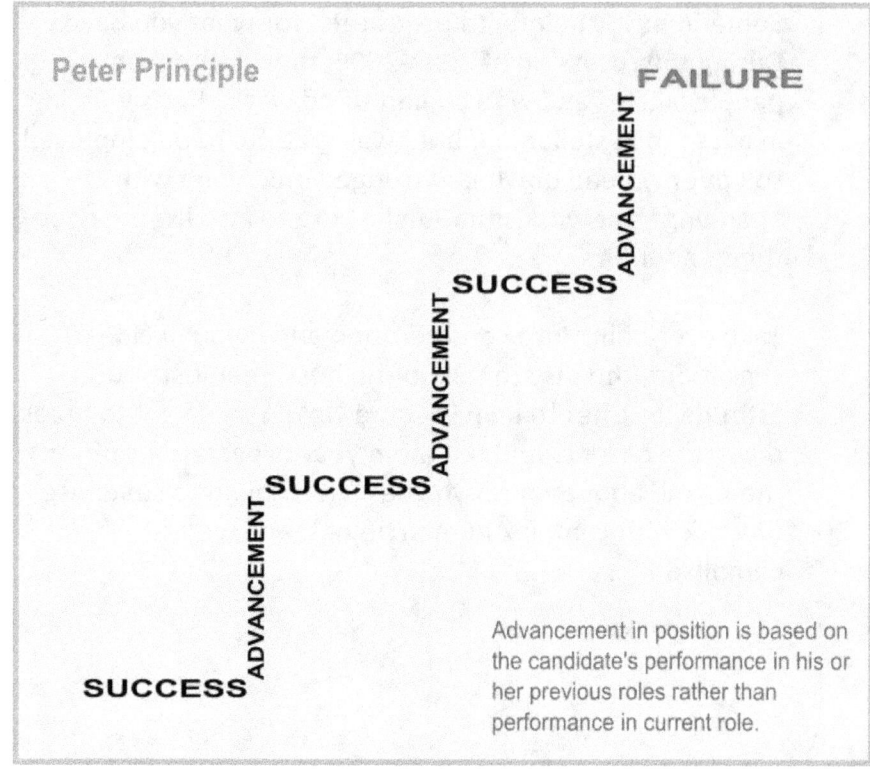

5. The Peter Principle is Valid

Management journals would not exist if managers were always perfect, so it's no surprise that *Harvard Business Review* has long been exploring the reasons behind manager incompetence and whose responsibility it is to compensate – the boss or the subordinate.

Nowhere was the problem stated more acutely, it could be argued, than in the wicked late 60s satire, *The Peter Principle*. Taking the form of a serious work of business research, complete with entirely fake examples, it purported to have discovered the root cause of manager incompetence: Everyone in an organization keeps on

getting promoted until they reach their level of incompetence. At that point, they stop being promoted. So given enough time and enough promotion levels, *every* position in a firm will be occupied by someone who can't do the job. The book struck a chord with the general public, staying on the *New York Times* bestseller list for over a year, and it's still in print almost 50 years later. (Andrea Ovans 12/22/14)
(https://hbr.org/2014/overcoming-the-peter-principle)
The Peter Principle was an observation put forth by Dr. Laurence J. Peter, a psychologist and professor of education.

Most of us have heard of the Peter Principle – where employees tend to rise to their level of incompetence and stay at that level for the rest of their careers. Have you ever noticed how most American companies select their managers?

They take the highest performing employees and tell them "Congratulations! You're great at what you do, so now you're going to train and supervise others!" By taking a more insightful view of this scenario we discover that being a great performing employee is totally different than supervising others. The skills don't necessarily transfer. Supervision takes an entirely different skill set. The criteria for what makes someone a really good salesperson or producer may not be the criteria that make a good boss.

How the Peter Principle Works
We live in organizations that are political, where favoritism, nepotism, and empire-building seem to be the norm. Many employees believe that somehow their hard work and loyalty will shine through and the big boss will

judge everyone fairly and promote the most qualified personnel into management. Unfortunately, it rarely happens that way because it's more about how you play politics and whether you tell the boss what he or she wants to hear, rather than being truthful. Are there really more bad bosses than good? Yes, probably.

I worked with car salespeople for years that were fantastic at selling vehicles, but were lousy at being managers. No one wanted to be the manager at one dealership I frequented so they were forced to take turns leading. It was partly because they made more money selling than managing. However, one day a "rotational" manager confided in me that he had no propensity for leadership. He didn't know how to motivate the sales team and was much happier when "his turn" at being sales manager was over for a few months. That way he could get back to a job where he excelled and felt comfortable doing. Many of them readily admitted their incompetency at leading and managing. The Peter Principle was alive and well at this dealership!

Peter also asserted that although people rise through the ranks of their organization by various means including being pushed or pulled by circumstances, or through the strategic help of well-connected players inside the organization, ultimately the ability to be promoted relies on the individual's competence at their current level. The more the employee exhibits competency in their position, the theory suggests, the more promotable the employee is for the next position in the hierarchy. Then eventually, through moving up the ranks, the employee is finally promoted from a position of competence to a position of incompetence.

The Peter Principle in Action
Take, for example, an excellent teacher. She's been teaching for ten years, had great rapport with students, uses innovative teaching methods, and has excellent peer reviews. They subsequently promote her to administration where she's required to do a lot of paperwork and is pulled away from teaching students altogether. She not only dislikes her new position, but asks to be moved back to teaching. However, the superintendent insists that she stay and "work her way" into the job. Unfortunately, her new positon came with a large salary increase and as time goes by, she gets accustomed to the higher salary, but not the job itself. She blinds herself to her incompetency and stays in that position until retirement.

This was a work tragedy, because she was taken away from teaching (the thing she loved most) and was an ineffective administrator. It cost the students, it cost her because of the stress she felt, and it cost the school district in wasting talented personnel.

It is clear that we all have our limitations, or shortcomings. That is why Dr. Peter's, *The Peter Principle*, makes intuitive sense and relates to us all. Have you sometimes felt that you've reached your level of incompetence? That you've gone as far as you can go? I like playing guitar and even formed a rock band in high school, but later came to realize that's probably as good as I'll get. I reached my level of incompetence, so now I play guitar to relax and express myself. Sure, I could take lessons and get better, but why?

You can easily find examples at work where people are in over their heads and have reached their level of incompetence. They could go for retraining or admit they feel uncomfortable and ask for help, but chances are they won't. Is it pride, not willing to admit they need help, or something else? Who knows?

Of course, the ideal solution would be that you're wise enough to know that you've reached your incompetence level and voluntarily step down to your previous position or ask for another position. After all, the company doesn't want to lose you and you were promoted for a reason. Unfortunately, in the real world, this scenario is unlikely to happen. It's human nature to strive for more and always progress, but wouldn't it be wonderful if we could all realize when we've reached our level of incompetence? That way we could step back to our previous position where we were highly effective and everyone would be more efficient in the organization.

One approach is to teach management skills to the technically gifted, but even that may not pan out. Technical skills are much easier to teach than soft skills such as active listening, empathy, respect, and leadership ability. There is no secret formula to being a good boss, but some people seem to have it and others don't. Great management is vital to an organization and leadership is personal. We are all incomplete human beings and there is no single style of leadership that will be successful in all cases. The key is making the effort to be a great boss and always improving your skills, whether it is through training or mentorship.

I like the Peter Principle because if used correctly, it could benefit organizations in big ways. For a good example, consider the top level of Maslow's need hierarchy, self-actualization. The employee strives to reach his or her potential by setting goals and overcoming challenges. They grow to better self-awareness and eventually come to the realization, after several promotions that they are in over their head. At this point, and this is the critical point, the astute organization will have the employee step back a level to where they performed admirably. This would strengthen all companies and lay the groundwork for having many more good bosses than bad. BUT, the critical juncture is interceding on the employee's behalf and moving them back to a position of competence and excellence. Unfortunately, companies do not do that for various reasons. The result being poorer bosses, higher turnover, and disengaged employees.

They will continue to muddle through and be ineffective. People will learn to go around them and they will never give up that position. They're making more money in the new position and don't want to step down for reasons of pride, reputation, or who knows? The company will feel the negative impact of their incompetence as well as impacting their subordinates. They won't be fired, unless they are extremely incompetent, and chances are they will try to maintain their position at all costs.

So what can we learn from this? What is the lesson here? **You may want to avoid getting promoted.** One of the greatest pieces of self-awareness is the knowledge that management, whatever its perks, might not be worth the burdens it will impose on you. Before you accept the new position, look deep inside yourself to examine not only if you're competent enough to take the promotion but also if you're willing and able to take on the additional responsibility. Will there be longer hours involved? More travel? How does your family fit in? Do you foresee the training will be adequate for you to learn new skills and apply them for the benefit of the company?   If you decline the offer, can you stay in your current job?

There's nothing shameful about deciding the promotion isn't for you. Many people do not want to supervise others. It's not written in stone that everyone must climb the corporate ladder. There is a lot to be said for an employee who finds his or her niche at the company and continues to thrive in that position. A happy, satisfying job is to be valued at any level.

Overcoming the Peter Principle
When someone gets thrust into a new and unfamiliar role the effects can be devastating for everyone involved. The manager is less productive, with lower morale and less innovation – and this can often have a knock-on effect on staff. When it comes to combating the Peter Principle, there are a few key areas where we find most organizations could enhance their efforts:

Promote more effectively: There's always room for improvement when it comes to career advancement and rewarding staff doesn't necessarily have to mean thrusting more – or different – responsibilities on them. Instead you could give performance related bonuses, involve staff in new projects they'd be good at, identify what skill set is needed and score employees in line with this.

Don't be afraid to demote: Changing an employee's role because they're under-performing can be a pain in regard to HR compliance and stifle morale for staff. But it can be worthwhile because failing to address these issues can lower the morale for an entire team or department. Demotion can be humiliating. It assumes that the person to be demoted is a valued employee who has simply wound up in the wrong job. The person is transferred to a new job, often in a different department, that may be a lower level position but doesn't have an obviously lower job title. This does more than save face. A pay cut can usually be avoided since salary levels often have wide overlaps. Ideally, the person also has been given the right job this time. Moving staff to roles that better complement their skill set can often be preferable, even if it is moving them to the same level rather than higher.
Review managerial duties: Identify the skills needed in the managerial role, compare with those of your candidate and highlight gaps. Then procure training to bring them up to speed rather than dunking them in the deep end. Promoting an employee because they're competent and productive shouldn't be a bad thing. Taking advantage of their current skills and molding them into their new role will encourage a better move to management.

Creating an effective management structure will help bridge any skills gaps that a newly promoted manager may have and therefore reduce any inabilities before they reach their level of incompetence.

There's no silver bullet when it comes to tackling this perennial issue, but by bearing the Peter Principle in mind, you can understand how to avoid pushing staff to their level of incompetence and recognize any staff that are in

danger of reaching theirs.
(http://www.gceducationandskills.ac.uk/news-events/news/overcoming-the-peter-principle)

Applying the Peter Principle Test
The Peter Principle book was written in the tone of serious business research, but it was actually intended as satire. The examples used in the book are fabrications. That didn't matter at all because the "principle" resonated with business people and managers who could see how it could absolutely be true. People do a good job and get promoted. It is only when they are not doing a good job when they fail to be promoted. So that is the role they stay in, often for a very long time. Eventually a company is full of people who are not good at their jobs.

Could your organization be an example of the Peter Principle? There are some ways to find out. Think through the following seven questions and apply them to your situation. Some comments are added about how Peter Principle organizations do things.

The Peter Principle Test

1. *Does your organization apply and measure performance at all levels, or just lower and mid-level people?*
   Peter Principle organizations are much more likely to objectively measure performance at lower levels, but then use subjective measures and impressions for higher-level employees.

2. *Does the average tenure of your employees rise from the bottom to the top of your organization chart?*
Peter Principle organizations are always stacked at the top with very long term people who rose into their roles over many years. Non-Peter Principle organizations tend to have tenured people all over the organization chart.

3. *Where is your professional development budget targeted, on entry-level, mid-level, or upper-level people?*
Peter Principle organizations tend to think of professional development as something for lower and mid-level people. High performance organizations expect everyone to keep getting better at what they do, especially leaders. This puts the emphasis on continual training needs, no matter the level in the organization.

4. *How long has the average manager in your organization been in their current role?*
Peter Principle organizations always seem to have managers in roles forever, eschewing cross-training and re-assignments. The organization then becomes stagnant due to expected routine behavior and no creativity flow. Continually maintaining the status quo can have detrimental organizational effects.

5. *Are promotions in your organization based on objective reasoning? Is the performance you are rewarding with promotions clearly measurable?*

Peter Principle organizations promote on seniority and loyalty (and sometimes favoritism), rather than performance, qualifications and demonstrated ability.

6. *What percentage of your managers and leaders were promoted from within your organization?*
Peter Principle organizations are far less likely to import leadership from other places. This "organizational nepotism" is a way of cementing the status quo and keep disruptive people out of the company.

7. *Has there been an uptick in employee complaints? Is turnover higher and morale lower?*
Peter Principle organizations have more of a tendency for high turnover because of bad, or incompetent bosses.

After applying these questions to your organization you'll have a good idea if your team may be at risk of being a Peter Principle organization.
(http://exceptionalleaderslab.com/applying-the-peter-principle-test/)

Tips for First-Time Managers
While the Peter Principle has not been proven in any scientifically verifiable way, we see anecdotal evidence of its truth everywhere. After all, have you ever secretly thought to yourself that your supervisor has no idea what she's doing? Or, have you ever wondered how the 200 hundred-year-old head of the company got to where he was, considering he falls asleep in meetings and seems otherwise completely clueless?

Here are a few tips based on experience:

1. **Don't assume authority until it is conferred on you from those on your team.** This is perhaps the most important lesson any person new to managing should learn. While someone above you had deemed it appropriate to leave you in charge of a handful of people, the people you will be working with on a daily basis probably had no say in the decision.
Even if you are technically above them on the hierarchical ladder, you do not truly become a leader until your employees see you as one. It is absolutely essential to curry favor with and gain respect from your colleagues before they'll listen to you.

2. **Listen carefully and always ask questions.** You can learn by listening to colleagues carefully and observing other managers who are skilled and respected. Main point: you can effectively avoid becoming a victim of the Peter Principle by making a commitment to learning from others.

3. **Get to know your teammates' strengths and weaknesses.** Make a genuine attempt to get to know everyone by meeting with each team member individually. Become acquainted with their personal work-related aspirations, their working styles, their weaknesses and any other information that will help you manage more effectively.

4. **Always own up to mistakes.** There's no escaping the fact that you are going to screw things up fairly often when you first start. The quickest ways to lose respect from your colleagues is to cover up your mistakes, pass the blame around, or simply just portray an image of yourself that you haven't yet lived up to. If you want your team to admit to their own mistakes and correct them, then you'll have to do the same yourself.

5. **Understand that you can't make everyone happy.** While being liked is an instrumental component of succeeding as a manager, you will often be forced to make decisions that not everyone will agree with. Don't kowtow to others' desires just because you want to please everyone. Assess every decision you make and by all means consult others' opinions. But in the end, once you've chosen a particular plan, stick to it until significant evidence demonstrates it's not working. (Angelita Williams 1/23/12) (https://www.brazen.com/blog/archive/on-the-job/overcoming-the-peter-principle-5-tips)

Why the Peter Principle Works
The following is an excerpt from Steve Tobak, CBS News MoneyWatch, 8/15/2011. In it, he explains why the Peter Principle is necessary and works:

Everyone's heard of the Peter Principle – that employees tend to rise to their level of incompetence – a concept that walks that all-too-fine line between humor and reality. We've all seen it in action more times than we'd like. Ironically, some percentage of you will almost certainly be promoted to a position where you're no longer effective. For some of you, that's already happened. Sobering thought.

Well, here's the thing. Not only is the Peter Principle alive and well in corporate America, but contrary to popular wisdom, it's actually <u>necessary</u> for a healthy capitalist system. That's right, your heard it here, folks, incompetence is a good thing. Here's why.
Robert Browning *once said, "A man's reach should exceed his grasp." It's a powerful statement that means you should seek to improve your situation, strive to go above and beyond. Not only is that an embodiment of capitalism, but it also leads directly to the Peter Principle because, well, how do you know when to quit?*

I mean, who turns down promotions? Who doesn't strive to reach that next rung on the ladder? When you get an email from an executive recruiter about a VP or CEO job, are you likely to respond, "Sorry, I think that may be beyond my competency" when you've got to send two kids to college and you may actually want to retire someday?

Wasn't America founded by people who wanted a better life for themselves and their children? Of course, there were plenty of indications that they shouldn't take the plunge and, if they did, wouldn't succeed. That's called a challenge and, well, do you ever really know if you've reached too far until after the fact?

You see, I sort of grew up at **Texas Instruments** *in the 80s when the company was nearly run into the ground by* **Mark Shepherd** *and* **J. Fred Bucy** *— two CEOs who never should have gotten that far in their careers.*

But the company's board, in its wisdom, promoted **Jerry Junkins** *and, after his untimely death,* **Tom Engibous***, to the CEO post. Not only were those guys competent, they revived the company and transformed it into what it is today.*

I've seen what a strong CEO can do for a company, its customers, its shareholders, and its employees. I've also seen the destruction the Peter Principle can bring to those same stakeholders. But, even now, after 30 years of corporate and consulting experience, the one thing I've never seen is a CEO or executive with an easy job.

That's because there's no such thing. And to think you can eliminate incompetency from the executive ranks when it exists at every organizational level is, to be blunt, childlike or Utopian thinking. It's silly and trite. It doesn't even make sense.

It's not as if TI's board knew ahead of time that Shepherd and Bucy weren't the right guys for the job. They'd both had long, successful careers at the company. But the board did right the ship in time. And that's the mark of a healthy system at work.

Nobody knows ahead of time if people are going to be effective on the next rung of the ladder. Every situation is unique and there are no questions or tests that will foretell the future. I mean, it's not as if King Solomon comes along and writes who the right person for the job is on the wall.

The Peter Principle works because, in a capitalist system, there are top performers, abysmal failures, and everything in between. Expecting anything different when people <u>must</u> reach for the stars to achieve growth and success so our children have a better life than ours isn't how it works in the real world.

The Peter Principle works. Want to know how to bring down a free market capitalist system? Don't take the promotion because you're afraid to fail. (https://www.cbsnews.com/news/why-the-peter-principle-works/)

Summary

In summary, the Peter Principle is valid, and can be overcome. It starts with the individual and comes down to four choices:

1. Stay in your position and muddle through. This will be costly for both the organization and your employees.
2. Seek training. You know where your weaknesses lie, so try to correct them.
3. Ask for your old job back. This will take courage on your part and will probably involve a demotion.
4. Do a self-evaluation. Look deep inside yourself and decide if you should actually accept or deny the new position.

Not everyone wants to climb the corporate ladder, though some people think that is what's expected of them. If you've found a position you're happy in, it is no disgrace to decline a promotion. If you fear the next promotion might be too much for you and your competency at doing the job would suffer, then decline the promotion. If you are a valued employee (obviously you are or they wouldn't have made the offer), making a good salary, and extremely competent, then the company will not force a promotion on you. If they do, it may cost them an excellent worker in the process.

6. What's Your Leadership Style?

In the early 1960s, Robert Blake and Jane Mouton wrote a popular book titled *The Managerial Grid*. The Leadership Grid (formerly called the Managerial Grid) is a model based on two important leadership-style dimensions: *concern for production*, plotted on the X-axis on a scale from one to nine points; and *concern for people*, plotted on the Y-axis on a scale from one to nine points.

The Leadership Grid
The model identified five leadership styles by their relative positions on the grid:

Impoverished (concern for production = 1, concern for people = 1)
Authority-compliance, sometimes called Produce or perish, or Task management (9, 1)
Middle of the road (5, 5)
Country Club (1, 9)
Team (9, 9)

The Leadership Grid demonstrates that placing undue emphasis on one area, while overlooking the other, stifles productivity. The model proposes that the team leadership style, which displays a high degree of concern for both production and people, may boost employee productivity.

Some of the perceived benefits of using the Leadership Grid include its ability to measure one's performance and that it allows for self-analysis of one's leadership style. Furthermore, it continues to see usage among organizations and businesses (https://www.investopedia.com/terms/l/leadership-grid.asp)

Let's take a closer look at the five leadership styles:

- 1, 1 **Impoverished Management**. In this leadership style the leader shows little or no concern for production and little or no concern for the employee (probably about to quit, retire, or no longer cares). When the leader does not wish to engage with his or her employees and lets them muddle on, this is a bad leadership style. However, this style can be a conscious choice. By giving employees the freedom to solve a specific problem, this will affect the production for a short while. But eventually, this will lead to independence and an improved production. When this leadership style is used overly much or continuously, Blake and Mouton recommend to take on a different leadership style.

- 9, 1 **Task Management**. The leader is completely focused on task-orientation. As the production is the leader's focal point of attention, he forgets and neglects the well-being of the employees. This leader is authoritative and exerts disciplinary pressure. The leader requires the utmost of the employees and imposes sanctions when they fail to meet the requirements. There are situations in which this style of leadership is necessary. For instance, when unpopular measures are taken like cutbacks or reorganization. The leader should not be afraid to show her human side from time to time, however.
- 5, 5 **Middle of the Road**. In this leadership style the '*happy medium*' course is adopted. The leader maintains a balance between the needs of the people and the production and the leader scores an average mark on both criteria. According to Blake and Mouton, this is not always an ideal leadership style but because of pressure of time such as meeting deadlines, it is a good way to encourage the employees.
- 1, 9 **Country Club**. Many new leaders orient themselves towards this style with a high concern for people but a low concern for production. In this style of leadership, leaders just want to be '*liked*' by their employees and they do not want to

come across as too authoritarian. The leader wants to understand her employees continuously and wishes to maintain a good relationship with them whatever the cost, with the risk that employees might cut corners and do not pursue the objectives enough. This leadership style may also be the leader's conscious choice. The moment an employee has to deal with personal problems the manager's care and support will be experienced as positive. It will temporarily affect the production but the backlog will be caught up at a later time.

- 9, 9 **Team Management**. The leader that is oriented towards this style should not change this. Her employees form a close-knit team and work together on the execution of objectives. The leader has a lot of respect for their employees and enthuses and motivates them. This is why they are able to bring out the best in themselves. Mutual involvement among the employees is high and they are very loyal to their employer. Such an optimal cooperation is often linked to short-term projects that are carried out by (highly) experienced employees. By paying a lot of attention to the needs of the employees and production needs, this leader works very efficiently (https://www.toolshero.com/leadership/managerial-grid-blake-mouton/).

Situational Leadership
A few years after the Leadership Grid's acceptance, another theory complemented the Grid, and makes intuitive sense. It's logical that the best leadership style be flexible, and Paul Hersey, in the late 1960s, theorized the

Situational Leadership Model. It is adaptive leadership that encourages leaders to assess factors such as: employee maturity level, readiness level, and the situation itself (task).

The key to the model is that the *boss adapts* his or her leadership style to the people, rather than expecting people to adapt to their leadership style. According to the theory, the most effective leaders are those that are able to adapt their style to the situation and look at cues such as the make-up of the group and the type of task. Leaders must be able to move from one leadership style to another to meet the changing needs of an organization and its employees.

The Situational Leadership Model was described as "organized common sense," by its creator. In addition to being flexible or adaptive, good bosses:

- Communicate expectations of the task or project and effectively influence behavior positively in the people they supervise
- Know what the group is capable of accomplishing as far as skill sets and individual employee strengths and weaknesses
- Assess employee readiness levels as to motivation, determination, enthusiasm, and attitudes. The leader must be able to assess the work group accurately if the tasks are to be completed successfully
- Determine maturity levels that will affect their leadership style. Are they experience? New hires? Will they need constant direction? What group members best fit with the task at hand?

For example, a successful Math teacher knows what level of Math their students can understand, and their willingness to learn. She doesn't start off with higher Math functions when they are struggling to just work fractions. She's a situational leader.

In summary, the Leadership Grid tells us what our preferred leadership style is, but the Situational Model emphasizes which leadership style should be used depending on the situation. The "situation" is a combination of such things as: employee readiness and experience, the leader's ability, and the task at hand.

Theory X and Theory Y
Part of our leadership style is reflected in how we view our subordinates. How do you view them? As equals, people who need whipping in shape, or as qualified employees who simply need guidance/coaching?
Social psychologist Douglas McGregor, realized the importance of managing people through more effective methods in the early 1960s, leading to his Theory X and Theory Y. He challenged management assumptions about how they viewed their subordinates. McGregor believed that too many managers assumed people were lazy and apathetic about work. He urged managers to realize there are employees who, under the right circumstances and leadership, are eager to perform well.

Assumptions of Theory X (pessimistic view of subordinates)

- An average employee inherently dislikes work and will avoid it whenever possible.

- Because of this dislike of work, most people must be persuaded, compelled, coerced, or even threatened with punishment to get them to put forth effort to achieve organizational goals.
- Employees prefer to be directed, dislike responsibilities, and resist change.
- Most employees value job security highly, but they have relatively little ambition.

Assumptions of Theory Y (optimistic view of subordinates)

- Employees will exercise self-direction and self-control for objectives they value.
- Employees will be loyal and committed to the organization if the job is satisfying.
- The average person learns, under the proper conditions, to accept and seek responsibility.
- Work is as natural as play or rest and they can be trusted.

Thus, we can say that Theory X presents a pessimistic view of employees' nature and behavior at work, while Theory Y presents an optimistic view of the employees' nature and behavior at work. When correlated with Maslow's hierarchy of needs theory, a logical comparison would be that Theory X is based on the employee wanting more physiological needs and safety needs; while Theory Y is based on the assumption that social needs, esteem needs, and the self-actualization needs dominate employees.

Implications of Theory X and Theory Y

First, many organizations use Theory X today. This theory uses control and supervision to achieve organizational goals. While it doesn't encourage creativity, there are instances where it can be applied. For example, Theory X leadership would be applicable in dangerous working conditions or where employees are new or on probation. Micro-managing can be used effectively in some instances, but should be used sparingly and only until acceptable performance levels are reached. However, if Theory X leadership is used too long, then employees become dissatisfied.

Second, many organizations use Theory Y today. Managers like to think they are Theory Y because they do trust and encourage employees to take initiative and to use self-control and self-direction. Theory Y bosses tend to utilize employee potential which meshes well with a flatter, or decentralized, organization where teamwork and good communication are highly important to organizational success.

Everyone believes Theory Y leadership is best and it usually is. However, I read an interesting case where that wasn't necessarily true. There was a pet food manufacturer in the Midwest where the plant manager was totally Theory X and after 20 years was moved to another manufacturing facility. His successor was a Theory Y leader so one might surmise the employees welcomed him with open arms, but that was not the case. After a short time, under his leadership, the whole plant nearly went on strike. Workers used terms such as "wishy-washy" and "uncaring," when describing their new plant manager. Corporate called in a management consultant to resolve the situation and after doing an employee survey and interviewing several workers, it was discovered that the previous manager was Theory X. He had conditioned workers over his 20 year tutelage not to think for themselves. He would give stern directions and employees soon became almost "mindless robots." They punched time clocks, knew they'd be given work assignments, and punched out at the end of the workday. They didn't have to think for themselves and were constantly micro-managed, which was a style they came to embrace. The new manager, being Theory Y, trusted workers to know their jobs and thought they needed little direction. When it came to light what was happening, production in the plant increased and the strike was averted. At last, employees were allowed to think for themselves. It seemed amazing that this could happen, because most people would relish being able to move from under a Theory X to a Theory Y boss.

Theory Z
Theory Z is a management approach by William Ouchi (1981) that complements McGregor's Theory Y style of leadership. Theory Z is centered on a combination of American and Japanese style leadership. Ouchi's premise is that of increasing employee loyalty to the company by providing lifetime employment. He also focused on the well-being of employees regarding their social life, using participative decision-making, concern for quality, and excellent transmittal of information. According to the theory, once the trusting relationship is established with workers, production increases. It is the responsibility of management to create an environment that lends itself to worker self-motivation.

Implications of Theory Z

- **Express your expectations**. Periodically, tell employees what standards of performance are expected. People need goals, but goals that are doable. This could include management by objective. The boss needs to take the time to meet with individuals and set joint goals, not just management demands. Then, the boss must follow-up with good communication, giving feedback and direction.
- **Make work meaningful.** When possible, assign people to the work they like and can do well. If it's meaningful and valuable to them, then it provides them an opportunity to grow, fulfill goals, and build self-esteem.
- **Make rewards and recognition a priority**. Different forms of positive reinforcement are keys to excellent organizational performance. Monetary rewards are important, but so are nonmonetary rewards. People like to be recognized for their good work.

Application of Theory Z

Ouchi's *first premise* of increasing employee loyalty by providing lifetime employment is not very relevant in our upwardly mobile society today. Nowadays, company loyalty is rare because historically part of the unspoken work contract was for the company to provide employment with the agreement that the employee would stay and give their best efforts. Unfortunately, through recessions, mergers, and restructuring, employees no longer feel loyal to organizations that lay off workers. So instead of giving their hearts and souls to the organization to climb the promotion ladder, employees are now looking elsewhere if they see no future with their current employer. In an effort to keep progressing, it's understandable that an employee who sees no growth with a company, or has a bad boss, would want to find another job.

However, Ouchi's *second premise* should be fulfilled. That is, to treat the employee with respect and provide them opportunities for participative decision-making, input, and goal achievement. Caring about the employee as a total person where the boss cares about their quality of performance, social life at work, and communicating timely information should not be underestimated. When employees are respected and cared about, they will return the respect and caring to their bosses and to the organization. Such thoughtfulness will build loyalty and provide bonding experiences for everyone. When the employee feels at home at work, and that work is satisfying, the organization will prosper.

What about Theory W?
I propose Theory W (for want of a better letter), which says that when you're first promoted to management, you are susceptible to moving towards Theory X from the get-go. You try too hard to have the best team in the company and toward those efforts you may micro-manage and constantly look over employees' shoulders for fear they're not doing their jobs well. You will probably be disliked by your employees until you realize, at some point, that they are competent to do good work. That's when you start letting loose of the reins. Initially, you are trying very hard to reinforce your boss' decision to

promote you into management. However, in your effort to impress your boss, you do not impress your subordinates. When the promotion wears off and you come back to earth, you'll move towards Theory Y style of leadership and become a better manager who is liked and respected by subordinates. It is then that you realize you work with good, qualified people and that by simply giving them direction, they will produce. It's a win-win, because you've become a more effective, caring manager, and they are more self-motivated employees. But, isn't it human nature to want to prove to everyone that you're the best manager the company has ever had?

The good boss has average turnover. The extreme of no turnover means that you're not grooming subordinates for promotions or helping them grow. Many times you can overhear bosses saying, "Oh no, I don't want to lose Cindy because she's too valuable to me." That's fine, if the boss is not holding Cindy back from progressing in the organization and she is happy in that position. But what if she's limited in salary range and aspires to more challenges? The good boss should have average turnover which is reflected in employees growing and progressing with the company. On the other hand, the other extreme would be lots of turnover, which indicates a poor boss.

As we've discussed, there is no "one best management style." It doesn't exist and management is situational. There are so many variables involved in leadership, but be yourself and be comfortable with yourself as a new manager. Give it time and don't try to make wholesale changes overnight because most people like routine and stability. Get your feet on the ground. People will give you a fair chance to prove your management skills and with experience and a positive attitude, you will be the caring, inspirational boss that employees rally around.

Summary

In summary, determine your leadership style and how you view your subordinates. Are they competent and experienced, or are they clueless? When you realize your leadership style, you can work to improve upon your shortcomings. Using the situational leadership model will help you meet people's needs at whatever the task and it will show your flexibility, which is an important trait in all good bosses. If they are new employees or on probation, you may lean temporarily towards Theory X style leadership to orient them properly or to correct bad habits. Of course, situational leadership calls for being flexible, and being Theory X temporarily is perfectly acceptable if the situation calls for it. However, the best bosses view their subordinates through Theory Y and Theory Z style leadership. Give employees the benefit of the doubt. Cut yourself some slack, try different approaches and you'll be rewarded with excellent employees.

7. The Evidence is In! Great Companies Have Great Bosses!

<u>What Makes a Company a Great Place to Work?</u>
No company has 100 percent satisfied employees. People will always find things to complain about. Even the most satisfying jobs in the world have a downside.

Positive workplaces tend to exhibit a common set of traits that foster excellence, productivity, and camaraderie. The best companies do have something over many other employers. Sometimes they are intangibles, and characteristics of a healthy workplace seem to have certain things in common, which include:

- Excellent communication. They share information with employees in a timely manner. Instead of dreading or trying to exclude input, they welcome feedback as an opportunity to grow. Companies treat employees as adults by informing employees, knowing they can handle negatives occasionally. We all understand the ups and downs of the organization, but communication, good or bad, builds trust.
- Treat respectfully and fairly. The company gives respect and in turn gets respect from employees. Employees who are dealt with fairly will be less likely to "pad" expense accounts or take things home from the stock room. They are paid well and want to do good work in return. The organization has substantial benefits and a good health plan. It uses layoffs as a last resort after every alternative has been exhausted.
- Delegate/train/trust. Managers delegate duties to subordinates, not just for menial tasks, but to develop and groom future managers. Training programs are at the forefront of the company, whether employees are salaried or paid hourly. Training allows all employees to competently deal with issues and represent the company well. Tuition reimbursement and mentoring opportunities provide employees pathways to success.
- Positive atmosphere. People enjoy working for a company that has positive values. Employees know they will have a supportive environment in which to work. Good attitudes abound and are grounded in worthy values. The "can do" attitudes result in better solutions to problems

whether within, or with customers. Positive reinforcement is alive and well and the company is ethical, honest, and straightforward in their goals of improving lives.

- Understanding. Work-life balance is emphasized and the company realizes that employees have lives outside of work. Its policies are flexible. It incorporates new technology and embraces employees learning new skills. Unless a crisis situation, overtime is voluntary and doesn't seek to impinge on an employee's home life.
- Sense of humor. Great companies and bosses keep things in perspective. Humor sends positive signals to the brain and relaxes the workplace, which makes it a more enjoyable experience for all involved. It also serves as an excellent stress release and keeps tensions from building. A good sense of humor can even help ward off illness. Laugh at yourself sometimes.
- Committed to excellence. Employees have a purpose, a mission to make their company the best. Management doesn't run down the competition but shows what it can do through having the best organization possible. Its customers, suppliers, and other stakeholders know what the company stands for because of its high interval values and standards.
- Teamwork. It's one for all and all for one. A feeling of camaraderie is a bonding experience that will keep productivity high and attitudes positive. Competition among groups is healthy and fosters cohesiveness. Employee support and cooperation is never underestimated. Great companies embrace the team concept.

- Good citizens. Good corporate citizens care about their communities by recycling and encouraging environmental awareness. They promote volunteerism by supporting charity and community efforts.

A company that's a great place to work is filled with great bosses. Employees are treated like adults, they are treated fairly, they are encouraged to grow in their careers and they are trained in how to do their jobs well. They work in a relaxed atmosphere where they have a purpose and are good citizens of the community. This is not by accident but by a designed company structure permeated with proper training, good communication, and respect. It is a positive corporate culture where people *want* to go to work!

Traits of Great Bosses
You're only as good as the people who work for you. A bad boss is any employee's worst nightmare. Whether they work at a Fortune 500 company or the local department store, employees want to work for someone who knows how to motivate people and encourage them to become even better.

- Go ahead, lose control. A boss that is controlling, who focuses on assigning busy work, who won't explain to employees what role they play, all of that is demoralizing. A good leader communicates to others the why's and wherefore's. They are not always right and they solicit input to enhance their decision making.
- Change is in the air. Many employees don't like doing anything that will require them to change;

however, for managers to resist change is putting jobs on the line in the long run. They educate and involve workers in the change process and the need for change.
- You're free to approach. The tactic of leading by fear makes employees uncomfortable. Are they supposed to regard their boss as some sort of ruler they cannot question? The good boss not only has an open door but they get out of their offices and associate with employees. They are approachable.
- They create visions. A boss who can't take the time to inspire with a road map to goals and visions will lock employees into dead end jobs. The good boss paints a picture of where the company is going and motivates people to follow.

Great managers make better decisions by studying the research, gathering/analyzing data, and using expert advice to make calculated decisions. They are also respectful, encouraging, even-tempered and innovative. Remember, bosses manage, but leaders lead.

<u>If You Want to be a Good Boss, Be a Good Leader</u>

1. **Build a bond of trust**:
   - Make sure that you're always honest. Always tell the truth, even if the news is good or bad, or it's to your disadvantage. Be transparent!
   - Be fair. It's easy to judge people based on their actions, but sometimes it's worth taking a closer look at their motives.

- Don't gossip and don't share anyone's personal information. Don't say bad things about employees who are absent.
- Show that you're a team-player and others can rely on you. Set a good example, finish your work on time and don't ask others to do the job you dislike.
- Be empathic. If you know that your employee is having a hard time, don't be afraid to ask them if they're alright or if they need any help.

2. **Praise your employees**. Recognition at the workplace cannot be underestimated. Look at some statistics: 16 percent of employees left their previous job due to a **lack of recognition**, 35 percent of them claimed that lack of recognition was the biggest hindrance to their productivity, and 78 percent of U.S. workers said that **being recognized** motivated them in their jobs.

How to recognize your employees:
- Thank the person by name.
- Specifically state for what they are being recognized.
- Point out the value added to the team or organization by the action that they have taken.
- Reward them with a gift (a dinner, tickets to a theater or a pay raise).

3. **Inspire your employees**. Inspiration at work is about commitment and passion. If your employees love what they do, they will need only a little bit of help from your side to spread their wings.

> How to inspire your employees:
> - Tell them about your vision – people love to know that they are part of something important.
> - Tell about benefits behind your ideas, don't speak only about "how" but tell them also "why."
> - Praise them and encourage them to develop.
> - Share your knowledge with them.
> - Acknowledge feedback!

4. **Let your employees be themselves**. If you don't accept your employees as they are, you cannot expect that they will feel comfortable in a workplace. If you want your employees to be highly motivated, you cannot increase the division between home and work. You need to integrate them.

> Let them be themselves:
> - If there is no need to look smart, don't try to implement a dress code.
> - Encourage them to talk about their passions.
> - Trust them and let them decide how to achieve their goals.

- Encourage them to take ownership of their work.
- Bring some joy to your workplace!

5. **Value feedback**. There are no perfect people as there are no perfect workers. That's exactly why you should encourage an open, honest communication in your company. Don't be afraid of it! Even if you hear something unpleasant, treat it as an opportunity to develop.

How to encourage employees to give feedback:
- Ask them questions. "What would you change if you were me?" "What do you like or dislike in your job?"
- If you don't want to speak in person, you can ask your employees to fill out a survey (it can be anonymous).
- Tell them honestly that if there is any feedback they would like to share with you, you'd be happy to hear it.

(https://www.livechatinc.com/blog/how-to-be-a-good-boss/)

Great Companies Lead the Way

There are many examples of great bosses running great companies. It's not about the bottom line; it's about how you treat your employees and customers. When the company focuses on employees, customers, and the surrounding community, it becomes self-sustaining and profit will never be a concern. Companies such as:

Google, FedEx Express, McDonald's, Facebook, Zappos, Costco, and SAS are consistently listed as best companies to work for. It's not by accident that they make such lists.

- Facebook. The social network company was founded in 2004 by Mark Zuckerberg. They may have found themselves on the receiving end of criticism of late regarding privacy concerns and political tampering, but that has not affected how its employees feel about toiling away in the tech trenches. Facebook has landed within the top 15 on <u>Glassdoor's Best Places To Work list for eight consecutive years</u>, securing the top spot in 2018. As CEO, Zuckerberg holds weekly question and answer sessions with non-executive personnel and emphasizes a workplace where cubicles feel at home and diversity and tolerance are engrained in the company culture. Employees are pampered with on-site barbers, bankers, bike shops, free dry cleaning, a company gym, and a shuttle service. Among other perks, the workers have unlimited sick days, three weeks paid vacation, free meals, and on-site health and dental care. (Facebook.com)
- Costco. CEO Craig Jelinek started from the bottom as a warehouse manager in 1984 and steadily rose through the ranks. He eventually took the reins from longtime big cheese Jim Sinegal in January 2012 and upheld his employee-friendly policies. Costco pays its hourly employees an average of more than $20 an hour and gives them overtime. Eighty-eight percent of the workers have company-sponsored health insurance and their premiums amount to less than 10 percent of the cost of their

plans. They rack up vacation time, paid time off, and sick days as they log more years with the bulk grocer, according to Glassdoor.com. "This isn't Harvard grad stuff," he said in an interview with Bloomberg.com. "If you treat consumers and employees with respect, good things are going to happen. People need to make a living wage with health benefits. It puts more money back into the economy and creates a healthier country. It's that simple." (Costco.com)

- Zappos. Who says work can't be fun? Certainly not the shoe empire's CEO Tony Hsieh. He built the online retailer around ten core values, which include "create fun and a little weirdness," "be humble," and "build a positive team and family spirit." According to CNBC, the company also runs on a "self-management" system known as "holacracy" so workers don't report to a direct manager and are empowered to have more input in decision-making. Zappos will give new hires a month's salary to quit if they don't love the job, which might be why they've been on *Fortune's* 100 Best Companies To Work For list for almost a decade. The positive environment extends to consumers, the less fortunate, and the Las Vegas community in which it is based. They host Thanksgiving dinner for those in need at their headquarters, partnering with charities like Soles4Souls, Kid In Need Foundation, and Spread The Word. They have one of the best return policies and large sections for inclusive sizing and adaptive clothing. When the financial crisis hit Vegas hard, Hsieh also invested $350 million of his own money to stimulate downtown revitalization

by buying 100 properties, creating an annual Life Is Beautiful Festival, and investing in small businesses and arts and culture. (Carrie Bell)
(Reprinted with permission from *Reader's Digest*) (https://www.rd.com/advice/work-career/companies-with-the-best-bosses-in-America)

From our examples, you'll notice a few things that great bosses, working for great companies, have in common:

1. **Great bosses are passionate**. Their passion shines through in their walk, their talk, and in their actions. They are excited about work. And that passion is contagious in lifting workers to higher levels of performance. In essence, great bosses are great role models.
2. **Great bosses coach**. While some bosses are quick to blame their employees, great bosses take it upon themselves and jointly work with people to solve problems rather than passing blame. Coaching is valuable because it gives people a sense of "we're in this together." If there is a mistake made, the great boss empathizes and assists the employee in learning from those mistakes. Great companies stress the importance of coaching, rather than directing and commanding.
3. **Great bosses know their employees**. The *management by walking around* concept is important to great bosses. They don't camp in their offices; getting to know employees is a priority. Unforgettable bosses know people individually. They know their individual strengths and weaknesses, what motivates them, their likes

and dislikes, and treat them as the unique individuals they are.

4. **Great bosses are genuine**. Sincerity, truthfulness, and timely communication are hallmarks of a great boss. They consistently follow through on things. They don't make false promises or try to cover up their mistakes. Great bosses acknowledge others' contributions and even apologize, if necessary. They are human, but they are genuine people.
5. **Great bosses keep their heads**. In crisis situations, the great boss takes the lead and forges on. They have self-doubts, but it doesn't show because they instill courage in us all. For example, the Apollo 13 mission was doomed to failure when a fuel tank exploded, crippling the spacecraft. The astronaut's lives were in grave peril. Flight director, Eugene Krantz, focused on solving the problem and lead mission control to successfully bringing all three astronauts home safely. There were great bosses at work during that space mission malfunction. Great bosses don't sit on their hands, or place blame; they roll up their sleeves and get to work solving the problem, thus inspiring others to do the same.
6. **Great bosses are team leaders**. They lead with humility and quiet strength. Everyone is an equal and worthy of respect so great bosses increase team cohesiveness. This helps teams work uncluttered and fosters innovation in decision making. The team is given timely information and any mistakes or problems are openly addressed.
7. **Great bosses are the total package**. They lead, they follow, they inspire, they protect, they teach, they care. We know great bosses are human, but

they seem to maximize strengths and minimize weaknesses in themselves and in those who count on them.

Summary

In summary, there is a common theme that runs throughout this book, and that is, training and education cannot be overestimated. Whether you're a new employee or just promoted to management, if you're not trained properly, your odds of being successful begin to dwindle. The company needs to step up because training the employee provides them with the competence to do the job correctly. Without training, the employee is left to sink or swim, which reflects back on the organization with higher turnover, no stability, lower morale, and higher costs. Everyone wants to do a good job and impress those around them but if they're not given the tools to do the job it will eventually affect the bottom line. It's beyond this author why the answer is so simple but companies don't follow through. The inefficiency of improper or no training is compounded when the employee has to inevitably be trained at some point, and that point comes after they've developed many bad habits because they were not taught differently.

Make use of employee surveys. The wealth of data will surprise the organization because people want to speak out about their jobs and conditions at work, but many are afraid that approaching the boss will have repercussions. An anonymous employee survey is a great report card on how the company is doing. It also shows employees that management cares about what they think. However, the organization needs to print results of the survey and possibly implement some of the suggestions or the employee survey will be quickly known as a feeble attempt to show that management cares when it truly doesn't. Morale will plummet.

Every organization should incorporate a management training program to ensure they have in place a pipeline of good employees coming up through the ranks, which in turn translates to providing good bosses who will lead the company into the future. Competition is at every company's doorstep and if people have to be subjected to bad bosses, they'll leave and devote themselves to a company that has good management and good training programs.

Finally, show your humanity by helping one another. For example, our college was expanding programs one summer by adding a culinary arts program, and the department chair asked for volunteers to work on Saturday. Tables, chairs, and equipment needed to be assembled and put up. He promised a continental breakfast for those who could help out. Unfortunately, only four people showed up out of 15, including myself. The department chair even brought his wife to help us. This was a bonding experience and as we worked together, I learned that the department chair had surgery three weeks before and yet he was willing to assist with everything. He said he still didn't have his stamina back, but worked for over three hours with us. I gained a whole new respect for our boss because he was willing to pitch in and help others, while many colleagues didn't care to show up. It was a simple thing, but spoke volumes regarding being a good boss, team player, and a caring individual. He demonstrated that he was a good boss!

8. I Can't Function This Way!

"I want to get along with my boss. I've been here for three years and I thought everything would smooth out over time, but the boss hasn't changed. I need to have a boss I can look up to, but he seems incompetent and we have to make up for all of his mistakes. He doesn't seem to know what he is doing! I tried talking to him and he was very vague and I'm afraid it's affected our relationship negatively, though I tried to use tact. He seemed to take it as criticism but I told him I just wanted to be a good team member and that we needed his guidance. He gets angry and my coworkers don't know what to do or how to handle it."

Now, frustration is setting in because you basically like your job but the boss is making it impossible. You've seen other people leave and those who stayed in touch with you said they were much happier at another company. It doesn't look like the boss will leave anytime soon via promotion or termination so you must take steps to protect yourself and your future. **Do not** give notice until you have other employment lined up, or at least a plan of action. You've invested too much to blow up one day in anger or frustration and quit when you don't have another job to go to. Plan what you will do and if you need to stay on for a while then put your head down and simply do your job knowing there are brighter days ahead.

Education is the greatest equalizer known. The value of education is not only bettering yourself but also gaining security and self-confidence in the process. If we limit ourselves to what's given to us, we are at the mercy of other people. But how do we break out of the "box" we are in at work when the boss won't listen or you don't like the work? Education! Go to school part-time at night or on weekends or take an online course. Take advantage of any on-the-job training seminars you can attend. That way you've acquired skills that will help you find a job you like. It will enhance your life in so many ways:

- You'll make wiser decisions
- You have a goal
- You're investing in your future
- You feel more positive about everything
- Your colleagues, spouse, and relatives support your efforts
- You'll gain new respect from others
- Achieving goals results in self-satisfaction
- You'll be rewarded, whether through promotion or acquiring new employment

This author took six years to obtain his Master's degree. That's okay. The company paid my tuition and I was able to go to school at night. I saw early on that I would not stay with the company and knew I wouldn't retire with them so I took advantage of opportunities they gave me. I had to drop out a couple of semesters because they were sending me out of town frequently, but I knew that was a small price to pay and it actually made me hungrier to finish the degree. By continuing my education I knew that I would be able to work elsewhere. So many people are held hostage by their company because they haven't upgraded their knowledge base, or skill set, and they are resigned to staying in a job they don't like. That's a shame!

A company doesn't intentionally try to lock you into your position, but to remain competitive they train employees to specialize. It's simply a matter of efficiency for the organization. You become very good at what you do, but you may not be able to get another job without a pay cut because of that specialization. Education is the antidote to that as it broadens your skill set and gives you confidence to move on, if needed.

It doesn't matter if you're subordinate or boss, if you've tried every way you can to do a good job but can't seem to be recognized, or you're just not happy, then the fundamentals are the same:

1. Educate yourself.
2. Take advantage of every opportunity for company paid training.
3. Keep your skills up-to-date.

Top 10 Reasons to Quit Your Job
You've done everything you can to make your current job work. But, it is just not working out. Whatever your reasons for why you can't make your current job succeed for you, it may be time to listen to your heart. You may find that it's time to quit your job. These are the top ten reasons why you might want to quit your job.

If any of these ten situations exist for you at your current job, they are difficult, if not impossible, to solve. You need to look out for your best interests. Your job consumes too many hours of too many days of your life for you to stay where you are—*miserable*.

It'll break your spirit and kill your soul if you go to work at a job that you hate every day. You'll make yourself miserable and possibly become the negative employee whom everyone avoids. Your unhappiness will flow over into your home life and affect your relationships with your family members and friends. Is it worth all of this? Of course not. Regardless of your situation, you owe it to yourself to find a job where you can be happy every day at work.

No excuses, now. If these issues exist with your current job or your employer, make a plan, conduct a job search, and change jobs. You can transform how you feel about work with the right job for you. If any of the following reasons are relevant to you, then you may need to make some important decisions.

1. Your company is experiencing a downward spiral, losing customers, losing money, and rumors of possible closure, bankruptcy, and failure prevail. Working every day is like waiting for the other shoe to drop. Senior company leaders are meeting behind closed doors. Even worse is seeing on the news that your company has issues and management never communicated that to their employees. Employees are fearful, looking for new jobs and the general environment is stagnant and anxiety provoking.

2. Your relationship with your manager is broken, damaged beyond repair. You have sought help to mend the boss relationship but you know it is too damaged for recovery. (Perhaps you were untrustworthy, missed work on too many days, or the manager acts like an untrustworthy jerk). Whatever the reason, the relationship is irrecoverably damaged. You need to take a hard look, maybe even talk to your manager about the situation. But, chances are, it's time to move on, time to quit your job.

3. Your life situation has changed. Perhaps you have married or had a baby, and the salary and benefits no longer support your life needs. You need to move on to better opportunities to support your family. Do this without regret after identifying that there are no new opportunities with your current employer that might change the situation.

4. Your values are at odds with the corporate culture. Perhaps your company is egalitarian and you believe in assigned parking spots for salaried employees. Your company does annual employee satisfaction surveys and you think these are a waste of time. Your company is hierarchical and you want to influence every aspect of your job. (Personal note: I worked at a company that sent a representative to each branch office to conduct employee satisfaction surveys and all of my co-workers were totally impressed that the company cared that much about how we felt and wanted our feedback. We hoped change was in the air and that they were finally going to listen. Unfortunately, we never got the final survey results. Many employees asked and never heard back—that's when we realized the company wanted to look as if they cared, but they truly didn't).

No matter where the clash is occurring, a lack of congruence with the corporate culture will destroy your attitude at work. Leave quickly once you identify this culture clash. The situation will not improve and sticking around may make you hate work.

5. You've stopped having fun and enjoying your job. No matter what changed in your workplace, when you dread going to work in the morning, it's time to leave your job. Just do some inner thinking about whether you are frequently resistant to change. It may not be the job if you have a long-term pattern.

6. Your company is ethically challenged. Perhaps, the managers lie to customers about the quality of the products or the day on which product will ship. You become aware that the company is stealing information from competitors. Whatever the issue, don't stay in an organization where your ethics are out of sync. Leave as quickly as you can if you have no way to influence more ethical behavior.

7. For whatever reason, you have behaved in ways that are considered improper at work. You've missed too many days of work, slacked off on the job, failed to maintain needed skills and just generally developed the reputation of a loser or a slacker. That reputation, once earned, is unlikely to change, so you might as well move on, while you have the opportunity.

8. You've burned your bridges with your coworkers. Your group is not getting along in an environment that requires people to work together well. Again, at some point, the reasons don't matter; start fresh in a new job and resolve to not let this situation happen again. Especially if your efforts to resolve the situation have been unsuccessful, it's time to move on.

9. Your stress level is so high at work that it is affecting your physical or mental health and your relationships with your friends and family. Watch for the signs of burnout and if they can't be cured, move on.

10. You are unchallenged, need more responsibility, and seek opportunities that just don't exist for you in your current organization. You've explored the current and potential options, and they are limited. You may be ready to quit your job when there are no opportunities waiting.

Ready to leave your job, or looking for ways to improve your current situation? Have golden handcuffs and feel that you are stuck in your current employment? It's time to move on.
Ready to quit your job? You can resign from your job in a way that reinforces your professional image and keeps current employer relationships positive. (Susan M. Heathfield, 5/12/17)

(https://www.thebalancecareers.com/top-10-reasons-to-quit-your-job-1919345)

Other Signs It's Time to Leave
Sometimes we aren't aware we're unhappy at our jobs until friends or family notice that we are irritable and complaining when almost every word we say is negative. However, some people thrive on negativity and complain, but don't seriously consider leaving their jobs. Most people don't live on negativity but are genuinely unhappy with their work situation. Here are some additional signs it may be time to find employment elsewhere.

- **You don't like who you work with.** Maybe some of your friends have left for greener pastures and you can't seem to get along well with the new crop of hires. Or, you've had some major disagreements with coworkers you thought were your friends. It just makes for a miserable experience when you can't seem to mesh very well with coworkers.
- **Complaining and stress have become a way of life.** Nowadays, stress at the job has been ramped up due mostly to technology and needing to do the job faster and more efficiently. You can't get away from the office because the boss has your cell phone number and it seems you're on call 24 hours. The company is setting unreasonable deadlines and the breakroom is filled with employee talk dominated by complaints and low morale.
- **You've lost your work-life balance.** You work as hard as the next person, but you'd prefer not to have so much overtime and working weekends is getting old. You would gladly trade overtime pay

for more time off. Even when you're not at the workplace, it's uppermost in your mind.

- **You don't play politics well**. When asked for input, you tell the boss and others how you truly feel rather than what they want to hear. Maybe you don't prefer to attend happy hour every Friday and "smooze" with the boss and others. Or, you don't joke with the boss the way that others do and you've been passed over for a promotion more than once.

- **At a dead end/pay isn't there/work isn't challenging**. You haven't had a raise in a while and one is not on the horizon. Your salary is acceptable, though you'd prefer to be paid more money for your efforts. The job is just not challenging anymore and has come to a dead end. You've considered a transfer but it would be the same job duties, just in another locale with no growth in sight. Plain and simple, you've lost your motivation. You are stagnant and feeling uncomfortable in the same daily routine. You are feeling close to burnout.

- **You question the direction of the company**. The organization recently lost some important clients and had to lay off a few people. It doesn't look like the company is growing and it may even be shrinking. There are new upper-level managers who don't seem to respect the way things have traditionally been and you may not want to hang around to see if the new regime will be successful. You're questioning everything from company reputation to the way it treats its workers to the types of leaders in the organization.

- **You've been blacklisted for any reason**. The company offered you a transfer to another city with no accompanying pay increase. After researching the cost of living at the new city, you've found the standard of living to be 20% higher in the new location. Since you're not getting a raise to be able to at least maintain your living standards, you refuse the transfer. Even as unreasonable as the offer seemed, they will probably never offer you another transfer.
- **Favoritism is running rampant**. The boss's son is now your boss. He's been with the company for a short time, is not qualified (doesn't have a bachelor's degree, though that's the minimum requirement for that position), and is a flake. You first wonder about nepotism and then are concerned that he has a very authoritarian management style. He doesn't take anyone's input and always feels he knows what's best for everyone. You then wonder if you can outwait him and maybe he'll move on to another department. Or, the boss flirts with pretty Maryanne so she gets the light work load while you're dumped on.
- **Sexual harassment or illegal behavior**. You've witnessed people joking that Sarah has the best legs in the office. Sarah's young and seems to eat up the attention, and enjoys wearing shorter skirts. But it is blatant sexism and sexual harassment. Or, your sales manager makes "sweet deals," to clients who are his friends by pricing at cost and making it up on other clients he charges the full price plus a markup. There may also be some bullying going on. Keep your eye out for another job. The aggravation isn't worth it.

- **Too many responsibilities**. There has been some consolidation of departments and they've continued to give you more and more to do. The boss told you months ago that it was only temporary, but your work load seems to increase weekly. They've not hired another person and you are getting tired of picking up the slack. You even enjoyed being the "go to" person for a while, but now it's getting old and nothing is changing to alleviate your situation.
- **Lack of communication**. Management never asks for input. There's never been an Employee Satisfaction Survey given since you started, even though it was a hot topic long ago. Unfortunately, research has found that upward communication is considered too time consuming by managers so they don't put forth the effort to get employee input. They always know best. For example, the company bought a new software package which was supposed to streamline things and it has bogged down the system terribly. It has cost the company some clients and management won't admit they may have made a mistake so everyone has to continue to muddle through a system that didn't deliver what the company said it would.

One final caution: don't let emotions rule. Sit down and write out a list of what you want in your ideal job. Then compare leaving vs. staying, and make sure the decision is grounded in facts and logic rather than in emotions and anger. How will this decision affect your family? Does the new job have potential? Will you be taking a pay cut to begin other work? Is the up side such that you'll make up the loss in pay in a short time? Can you transfer? Do you want to? Do you think you'll like the new people and the company? We all get upset at our workplaces but if you make a rash decision to quit then and there, chances are you'll regret it. Every workplace has its downside so don't expect to find the perfect job, but do your research and ask questions to give yourself the greatest chance of finding that one great job for you. Always try to have another job to go to before giving notice because it will make you easier to employ.

You've Decided to Leave, Now Comes the Exit Interview
When you quit a job, there's a good chance HR will ask you to partake in an exit interview.
People tend to have mixed feelings about these conversations. Some say an exit interview is the ideal opportunity to be completely honest about your experiences with your employer and offer them critical and constructive feedback; while others argue it's awkward and not worth the risk of burning bridges, as your criticism probably won't inspire any significant changes anyway.
But regardless of your attitude toward the exit interview, it's imperative that you be cordial and professional.

"This could be the last impression you'll leave your employer with," says Michael Kerr, an international business speaker and author of *You Can't Be Serious! Putting Humor to Work*. "And don't think this conversation doesn't matter since you're leaving anyway. People talk. It's your reputation and your personal brand on the line. And those will travel with you wherever you go."

You also never know when you'll work for that HR manager or boss again. "I can't tell you how many boomerang stories I've heard where employees return back to their former employer after a year or two, or even wind up working with those colleagues elsewhere," Kerr says. "No matter how certain you are you won't return or come in contact with these people again, *never* burn bridges."

Here are 18 phrases you should avoid in every exit interview:

"I never really liked [coworker]," or, "[Name] was never very nice to me."
Don't get personal. "Attacking certain managers or employees will only reflect poorly on you, and make you come across as bitter or vengeful," Kerr says. "It's okay to discuss some behaviors that you feel had an impact on your decision to leave, but resorting to name calling or character assassination will never get you far and will only make it look like *you* were the difficult person to get along with."

"My boss was the worst because..."
Lynn Taylor, a national workplace expert and the author of *Tame Your Terrible Office Tyrant: How to Manage Childish Boss Behavior and Thrive in Your Job*, says you must remember that just because you're not speaking directly with your boss, doesn't mean you should lose your cool or make any last-minute snarky comments. "By being *too* honest about your manager you can shoot yourself in the foot if you ever want to return to the company, or expect a good reference from that boss," she says. "Remember to keep your comments general, concise, and make them overall positive."

"This place is a sinking ship."
"Why do people feel compelled to make remaining employees feel badly just because you are moving on? I don't get it. But stop it," says Dana Manciagli, a career expert and author of *Cut the Crap, Get a Job!*

Kerr agrees. "Never wish them poor by saying things like, 'I hope this company dies a slow, painful death.' If you are leaving on bad terms you may feel this deep inside, but using your outside voice to express this is a big no-no that will only serve to make you look petty and spiteful, and it will say more about you than it does about the company."

"I heard [name] did [xyz]," or, "[Name] was actually the one responsible for that error."
Don't gossip, and definitely don't throw your colleagues under the bus. It's unprofessional and unkind.

"I was really amazing at this job," or, "Good luck running this business without me."
Don't gloat about how fabulous you were, thus implying that it's a huge loss on their part, Kerr says. The time to boast a bit may have been on the way in, not on the way out. "It's fair to say that you felt like your talents weren't being used fully and to offer examples, but it's not wise to tell them you were the greatest thing since sliced bread and they're going to be sorry after you're gone."

"No comment."
Now's not the time to be curt, non-responsive or offer a terse, "no comment." "Being evasive or tight lipped will only make it seem as though you are hiding something and not cooperating with the process," Kerr explains.

"This company's pay is not market-competitive," or, "I'm leaving because I was offered a lot more money elsewhere."
Don't make it about money. "A statement about your compensation, even though it may be true, will be perceived as a negative slam against the company in your future career endeavors," Taylor says.

Manciagli agrees: "Unless you have done a statistically sound market study, then you do not know if your pay was market-competitive."

"I never really liked where I sat," or, "The printers never worked."
Don't focus on trivial matters, Kerr says. "Focusing on minor, trivial items will make you appear high maintenance and be viewed as wasting everyone's time. Instead, offer constructive ideas on larger systemic issues that you feel might have a serious and lasting impact on the culture."

"This is the worst company I have ever worked for."
"You're basically nailing the coffin shut on any opportunity to return to that company, or have the company be a positive reference," Manciagli says. "There is no upside to bashing the company you are exiting. None."

Taylor says your time to try to change things and communicate any issues you had was during your employment, not as you leave.

"My new job/company is amazing."
"Don't minimize your former employer by bragging about how you're moving onto much bigger and better things,"

Kerr advises. "It's great to be positive about the future and show enthusiasm, but don't do it in such a way that comes across as a backhanded compliment."

"I think [name] is really unhappy here," or, "Nobody is happy here."
Don't speak for others. "This can hurt you in the eyes of people who may have shared confidences with you," Kerr says. "Just make this about your story, no one else's."

Also, don't try to suggest the ship is going down with you. "Even if it's true, your coworkers won't appreciate it, and you're not their spokesperson," Taylor says. "If they're about to jump ship, that will be their task."

"I'd never work here again"
"If it was so miserable for you while you were earning a paycheck and benefits, then why did you stay?" Manciagli asks. "Every employee has choices to make. I don't see bars on the windows and doors or your feet chained to the floor. Yet now, because you are on your way out, you disclose it was that bad. A little dramatic for my taste and makes you look totally unaccountable for your own career."

Plus, remember that your last day is rarely the last affiliation you'll have with your employer.

Kerr says it may be difficult to find the right balance between being honest and cordial, especially if you've got any pent up anger or frustrations — but he says if you frame your opinions in such a way "that you are first and foremost thinking about what's best for the company, you'll have a far greater chance of having a real impact and

leaving a more positive impression." (Jacquelyn Smith 9/17/14)
(http://www.businessinsider.com/never-say-these-things-during-an-exit-interview-2014-9)

Finally, think positive. You will be through with this company when your exit interview is concluded, so take the attitude that you're happy to be leaving and moving on (though don't say that out loud). Suggest ways the company might improve without making your comments too personal. Talking constructively will make you look professional, whether or not they take to heart what you say. There's no need for a personal vendetta against your boss because they are well aware of who your supervisor was. You've discovered this job or company is not for you so take the high road and wish them well—you can celebrate when you get home.

Find an organization where you'll be happy and can grow, not only with the company but as an individual as well. It makes no sense to stay in a job you dislike just because the money is good. Chances are you'll pay for it in the long run through unhappiness, stress, and health concerns.

Summary

In summary, you've tried everything possible to like your job, but it's just not working. You've talked to the boss, to no avail, and you like your coworkers but you're stressed all of the time and not sleeping well.

Many of us don't like to give up and hope that the boss and/or situation will improve. But look at yourself honestly in the mirror. Is there anything further you could change on your part? If not, it's time to throw in the towel and leave with a clear conscience.

Unless you're one of the idle rich, always have other employment lined up before giving notice to your current employer. Or, at the very least have a plan that you've thought through thoroughly. Go through the exit interview with a positive attitude of helping the company and the coworkers you are leaving behind. Then, walk out of the building with your head held high, knowing a brighter future awaits.

Reasons to stay:
You love your job
You don't like your boss, but he or she will be leaving soon (for whatever reason)
You're coworkers are like family
You see a bright future if you can get through a few months of turmoil
You are growing, inside and outside of work
You respect what the company does and stands for
You would like to be promoted to management someday

Reasons to leave:
Bad boss and there's no hope of change
They don't seem to care about training you properly
Many coworkers are leaving
Negative atmosphere (due mainly to bad boss)
You don't want your boss's job
You don't see yourself retiring with this company
Much bending of rules and ethics
Favoritism, nepotism, politics, power trips, arbitrary policies

9. Final Summary

Be a good boss and then strive to be a great one! But it is rare to find a great boss. This author has been lucky to have worked with two good bosses, but the bad bosses were easily in the majority. Any company should want to have all good bosses because it helps perpetuate the organization. It provides a competitive advantage when a company has lower turnover, a more productive and efficient workforce, happy and satisfied employees, continued growth, and a good reputation in the community. That's a company that people will clamor to work for.

It is my wish to emphasize four main concepts throughout this book that are of critical importance to being a good boss, then a great boss. They are **communication**, **compassion**, **motivation**, and **training**.

Communication is critical at all levels of the company. Employees want to feel a part of the company and communicating both good and even bad news creates a culture of trust and loyalty. Everyone longs to know what's going on in the company, and open and honest communication fulfills that need.

Giving information after the fact or hiding information can hurt morale and tells employees that management doesn't care enough to let them know what's going on around them. If the grapevine is running rampant with rumors concerning company issues then the organization is not healthy because management is not communicating core information. The grapevine should only carry gossip, not rumors of layoffs, for instance.

Compassion is not weakness. In fact, it's a strength that shows the employee that you care. You empathize and realize where workers are coming from and try to find solutions to issues that crop up on the job. It's caring about them as individuals and treating them the way you'd like to be treated (Golden Rule Management).

A boss with tunnel vision, who strictly adheres to rules and procedures, is missing an opportunity to show they are human. Unforeseen things happen in life and the boss who doesn't recognize that fact may lose a good employee. Sometimes the rules can be bent temporarily for the good of employees.

Motivation is powerful. The boss who can move people to action and instill self-direction is a great boss! Most bosses don't know how to motivate and all too often think it's money that keeps us coming back. A boss who tries to motivate employees may make mistakes, but employees appreciate the effort and will respect the boss who does try. A great boss always tries to motivate.

The boss who isn't motivated themselves or who is not interested in motivating others will never be a good boss. They need to be retrained and learn motivation theories and tactics to better reach employees.

Training an employee fully and properly sends so many positive signals that will help make the organization great. It tells individuals that the company cares enough about them that they want them to have the competence to do their job. Excellent training is the cornerstone for success, both for the employee and for the company. It is the launch pad for employee growth and loyalty. Self-esteem, recognition, self-confidence, caring, and respect are important byproducts of training. Training never stops. Everyone from first-line employees to upper level management needs skills updates to remain good employees and keep the company competitive.

Poor, or little, training will diminish spirits because employees learn that they have to fend for themselves. This breeds bad bosses and people put in leadership positions that are unqualified, which can have a devastating impact on the organization. The employee who is poorly trained develops bad habits that will be expensive and time consuming to correct down the road.

A great boss:
- Listens
- Cares about their employees
- Communicates well
- Disseminates timely information
- Is trusted and trusts employees
- Is respected and respects employees
- Is qualified
- Doesn't gossip
- Supports employees
- Trains employees and makes further training available to keep skills updated
- Encourages questions
- Helps employees grow
- Gives raises as soon as an employee deserves it
- Is a good role model
- Explains policies and procedures
- Avoids tunnel vision and sees the big picture
- Empathizes

- Has a sense of humor
- Accepts the employee's word
- Is fair
- Gets to know employees
- Represents the company well
- Is even-tempered
- Remains calm in crises
- Has a positive attitude
- Never stops trying to motivate others
- Is motivated themselves
- Is also a good leader
- Doesn't abuse power
- Interprets new policies and procedures from upper management
- Praises and recognizes good work
- Praises in public, criticizes in private
- Gives timely feedback
- Doesn't demand
- Is approachable
- Uses interpersonal skills to build up rather than tear down
- Keeps confidential information confidential
- Tells the truth
- Is genuine
- Keeps promises
- Is a team player

This is a long list of qualities, but not anything a great boss wouldn't be able to accomplish. It's worthwhile and it's doable. Being a great boss is not for sissies because it takes dedication to want to be someone who can influence others for the better, inside and outside the organization. The need for power should not be underestimated, but when a great boss acquires that power they use it to influence and change the company positively.

In summary, aspire to that promotion you've worked hard for! It's been a long road but you're in a position to better things for people around you. Hopefully, you'll be going through a management training program and learn valuable tools to contribute to organizational success. If, for some reason there is not a thorough training program in place, gird your loins and do whatever it takes to be a great boss. Find a mentor, ask questions, listen and observe, read management books and learn motivation theories. Take time to map a plan for goals you have for yourself and your department.

At this point in your career you probably know your leadership style, so play to those strengths but strive to improve weaknesses. Are you more task- or people-oriented? Can you flex between styles to match your subordinates style and situation? Your challenge is to be a boss that sets the standards in the organization with compassion and caring and employee's will be lining up to work for you. Lead the way!

www.ingramcontent.com/pod-product-compliance
Lightning Source LLC
Chambersburg PA
CBHW071549220526
45469CB00003B/955